IMAGES OF THE CI
IN WEST VIRGINIA

R

By Terry Lowry & Stan Cohen

HEADQUARTERS
28TH OHIO VOL.
GAULEY BRIDGE,
W. Va.

QUARRIER PRESS CHARLESTON, WEST VIRGINIA

Charleston, WV

10 9 8 7 6 5 4 3 2

Printed in the United States of America

Library of Congress Control Number: 00-134149

ISBN 10: 1-891852-12-4
ISBN 13: 978-1-891852-12-1

Cover graphics: Egeler Design
Layout: Stan Cohen
Typography: Jan Taylor

Distributed by:

West Virginia Book Company
1125 Central Avenue
Charleston, WV 25302
www.wvbookco.com

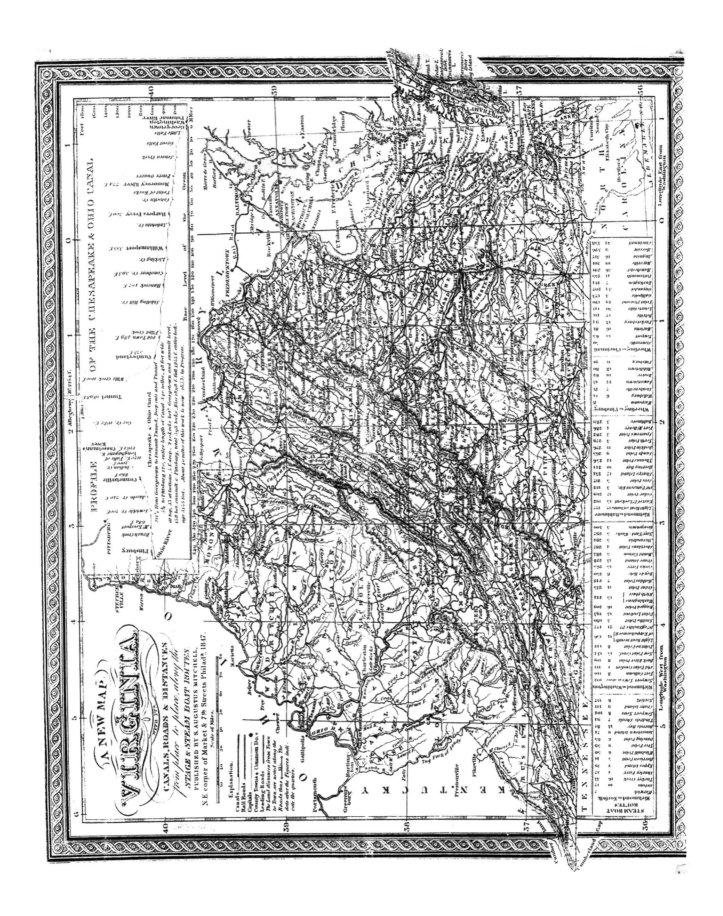

A NEW MAP OF VIRGINIA WITH ITS CANALS, ROADS & DISTANCES from place to place along the STAGE & STEAM BOAT ROUTES. PUBLISHED BY S. AUGUSTUS MITCHELL. N.E. corner of Market & 7th. Streets Philad.a 1847.

Introductions

Twenty-four years ago I published my first book *The Civil War in West Virginia, A Pictorial History.* I attempted to collect as many original photographs and drawings as I could along with photographs of historic sites as they appeared a century later. In the ensuing years I published Civil War books for the major Civil War authors of the state—Terry Lowry, Tim McKinney, Jack Dickinson, Joe Geiger and Bill Wintz. In addition I published, along with Wintz and Richard Andre, *Bullets and Steel, The Fight for the Great Kanawha Valley, 1861-65.*

With each book publication, more and more contemporary photographs and drawings surfaced through the years. The popularity of local interest Civil War books flourished.

Although the state's terrain precluded the major battles that were occurring in the east and west and limited the ability of photographers to roam the country, a remarkable number of images have been found. Additional drawings were found in the major news magazines of the day such as *Harper's Weekly, Frank Leslie's Illustrated Newspaper* and *The New York Illustrated News.* Archives throughout the country were searched to find as many images as possible.

Many never-before-published photographs are presented here along with many that have been published in books and magazines. My coauthor Terry Lowry and I decided that it was time to reproduce all of these in one volume for a handy reference for Civil War buffs, in and out of the state. It is an undertaking that we will continue even after publication of this book to add additional finds to subsequent reprints.

We know of some images we were unable to get copies of in time for this book, and there are probably many more that are just waiting to be discovered. We would like to encourage the public to contact us as new images are located.

Because of the number of images available, we are limited in the scope of this publication to include only those that were created from 1860 to 1865. With a few exceptions, we purposely did not include individual portraits of personalities. We did, however, include post-Civil War photos of the men who fought the war in a chapter entitled "Carrying on the Memories." Contemporary broadsides and some interesting paper items are also included, but this chapter is far from a complete collection. The first chapter on statehood is intended to give the reader an understanding of why the state was formed and the conflicts that occurred.

We would also like to stress that many of these images are of poor quality but have been used for their historical value. This is understandable due to the aforementioned nature of the state's geography, the early state of photographic processes, the drawings done by soldiers and civilians on scene and the fact that these are all over 130 years old.

Stan Cohen, Coauthor and Publisher

A mutual love of the visual image during the Civil War, both photographic and artistic, drew me to Stan Cohen as a publisher for my first book in 1982. Throughout the ensuing years, and in collaboration with many others, we have located numerous previously unpublished as well as published images of the Civil War in West Virginia. As a result of these efforts we often talked of publishing the definitive book of these images, photographic and artistic, made in and of West Virginia during the Civil War. Individual portraits and Harpers Ferry were to be excluded as available images of those two subjects could fill an entire book. Therefore, we decided upon a small sampling of those two areas. We also included veteran reunions and miscellaneous paper items. Broadsides which were in the original plan, are also to be found.

Regretfully, it was impossible to include all images as we originally envisioned. For instance, we were unable to locate a complete run of *The New York Illustrated News,* therefore, a number of the missing issues may well contain West Virginia views. Compounding this problem was that the images we did use from this publication had to be taken from microfilm which lends to poor reproduction quality. Along similar lines, *Harper's Weekly* and *Frank Leslie's Illustrated Newspaper* also contained some images we did not use.

Some images, such as a soldier's drawing of a Confederate camp of the Wise Legion on Sewell Mountain, Fayette County in 1861, could not be used as it was drawn on crude blue paper and could not be clearly reproduced, despite the best efforts of its repository, the Virginia Historical Society at Richmond. A similar situation existed for a photo at the Georgia State Archives believed to be of some officers of the 12th West Virginia Infantry. Some private collectors did not wish their holdings to be published, although they assisted us in many other ways.

Another deterrent to some images was the high use fee charged by their owners, which explains why we did not use all the paintings of W.D. Washington. And although we mention David Hunter Strother, we did not use any of his sketches as most are of activity in the Shenandoah Valley.

Despite such shortcomings, we have probably unearthed about 85 to 90 per cent of available images and hope to include more in the future.

Terry Lowry, Coauthor

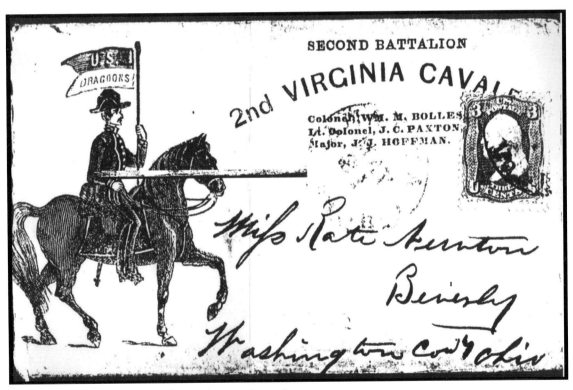

2nd (West) Virginia Cavalry regimental envelope. WASHINGTON COUNTY HISTORICAL SOCIETY

Many people through the years have helped with this project. We obtained images from the following for which we are extremely grateful:

- Mudd Library, Oberlin College, Oberlin, Ohio
- Emory University, Atlanta, Georgia
- Donald Rice, Elkins, Randolph County Historical Society
- Thomas Koon, Fairmont, Marion County Historical Society
- Bill McNeel, Marlinton, Pocahontas County Historical Society
- Carolyn Parsons, Museum of the Confederacy, Richmond, Virginia
- Bob Conte, The Greenbrier Resort
- Bill Wilcox, Huntington
- Larry Syplot, Morgantown
- The Rutherford B. Hayes Presidential Center & Library, Fremont, Ohio
- The New York State Archives, Albany / Ann Aronson
- Susan Collins, Jefferson County Museum, Charles Town
- University of California, Los Angeles, Special Collections
- Debra Basham, Archives and History Section, The Cultural Center, Charleston, West Virginia
- Staff of the West Virginia and Regional History Collection, Morgantown
- National Society of Colonial Dames of America in West Virginia
- Olive Crow, Anna Jarvis Birthplace Museum, Webster
- L.M. Strayer, Dayton, Ohio
- Richard Andre, Charleston
- Ronnie Ann Tront, Dearborn, Michigan
- Harrison County Historical Society
- Steve Cunningham, Sissonville
- Staff of the Harpers Ferry National Historic Site
- Carnifex Ferry State Park
- Library of Congress, Washington, D.C.
- Blennerhassett Historical Park Commission, Parkersburg
- Baltimore & Ohio Railroad Archives, Baltimore, Maryland
- Tim McKinney, Fayetteville
- Jack Dickinson, Huntington
- Hunter Lesser, Elkins
- Bill Wintz, St. Albans
- Charles Bracken, Charlton Heights
- Kjysten W. Drew, Salines, California
- U.S. Army Military History Institute, Carlisle, Pennsylvania
- Ellen Dunable and Margaret Brennan, Wheeling
- Mineral County Historical Society
- Dave Moore, Charleston
- Rob Wolford and Dave Pancake, Romney, Hampshire County Historical Society
- Everett K. Cooper, New Cumberland, Pennsylvania
- U.S. Forest Service, Elkins
- University of Illinois, Champaign, Illinois
- Emory Kemp, Wheeling
- National Archives, Washington, D.C.
- City of Philippi
- W.T. Lawrence, Fayetteville
- Barbour County Historical Museum
- Hardy County Library
- James E. Morrow Library, Marshall University, Huntington
- Brian Kesterson, Washington, West Virginia
- Virginia Historical Society, Richmond, Virginia
- Washington County Historical Society, Matietta, Ohio

Chronology of Military Actions in West Virginia, 1861-65

1861

May 30	Grafton occupied by Confederates
June 3	Battle of Philippi
June 19	Skirmish near Keyser
July 2	Skirmish at Falling Waters
July 4	Skirmish at Harpers Ferry
July 7	Skirmish at Middle Fork
July 7	Skirmish at Glenville
July 8	Skirmish at Belington
July 11	Battle of Rich Mountain
July 12	Beverly occupied by Federals
July 13	Battle of Corrick's Ford
July 13	Romney occupied by Federals
July 15	Harpers Ferry evacuated by Confederates
July 16	Skirmish at Barboursville
July 17	Skirmish at Scary Creek
Aug. 25	Skirmish at Piggot's Mill
Aug. 26	Skirmish at Cross Lanes
Sept. 2	Skirmish at Hawk's Nest
Sept. 10	Battle of Carnifex Ferry
Sept. 12	Skirmish at Cheat Mountain Pass
Sept. 13	Skirmish at Cheat Mountain
Sept. 14	Skirmish at Elk Water
Sept. 16	Skirmish at Princeton
Sept. 24	Skirmish at Hanging Rocks
Sept. 24	Skirmish at Mechanicsburg Gap
Oct. 3	Skirmish at Greenbrier River
Oct. 16	Skirmish at Bolivar Heights
Oct. 26	Romney occupied by Federals
Nov. 10.	Skirmishes at Blake's Farm and Cotton Hill
Nov. 10	Battle of Guyandotte
Nov. 12	Skirmish on Laurel Creek
Nov. 14	Skirmish near McCoy's Mill
Nov. 30	Skirmish near the mouth of Little Capon
Dec. 13	Battle at Camp Allegheny
Dec. 29	Sutton occupied by Confederates

1862

Jan. 3	Skirmish at Bath
Jan. 3	Skirmish at Huntersville
Jan. 4	Skirmish at St. John's Run
Jan. 4	Skirmish at Slanesville
Jan. 7	Skirmish at Blue's Gap
Jan. 11	Romney occupied by Confederates
Jan. 14	Logan burned
Feb. 2	Skirmish at Springfield
Feb. 8	Skirmish at mouth of Blue Stone
Feb. 12	Skirmish at Moorefield
Feb. 14	Skirmish at Bloomery Gap
Mar. 3	Skirmish at Martinsburg
May 1	Skirmish near Princeton
May 1	Skirmish at Camp Creek
May 7	Skirmish near Wardensville
May 16	Princeton occupied by Confederates
May 17	Princeton occupied by Federals
May 23	Battle of Lewisburg
May 28	Skirmish near Franklin
July 25	Skirmish at Summersville
Aug. 6	Skirmish at Pack's Ferry
Aug. 7	Skirmish at Horse Pen Creek
Aug. 18	Skirmish near Corrick's Ford
Aug. 30	Buckhannon occupied by Confederates
Aug. 31	Weston occupied by Confederates
Sept. 1	Glenville occupied by Confederates
Sept. 2	Skirmish at Spencer
Sept. 11	Battle at Fayetteville
Sept. 13	Battle of Charleston
Sept. 20	Skirmish at Point Pleasant
Sept. 27	Skirmish at Buffalo
Sept. 30	Skirmish at Glenville
Oct. 1	Skirmish at Shepherdstown
Oct. 6	Skirmish at Big Birch
Oct. 20	Skirmish at Hedgesville
Oct. 31	Skirmish near Kanawha Falls
Nov. 9	Skirmish at South Fork
Nov. 26	Skirmish at Sinking Creek
Dec. 3	Skirmish at Moorefield
Dec. 12	Skirmish near Bunker Hill

1863

Jan. 3	Skirmish near Moorefield
Feb. 12	Skirmish near Smithfield
March 7	Skirmish at Green Spring Run
March 28	Skirmish at Hurricane Bridge
March 30	Skirmish at Point Pleasant
April 5	Skirmish at Mud River
April 20	Start of Jones–Imboden Raid
April 24	Beverly occupied
April 25	Skirmish at Greenland Gap
April 26	Skirmish at Rowlesburg
April 27	Morgantown occupied by Confederates
April 29	Buckhannon occupied by Confederates
April 29	Fairmont occupied by Confederates
April 30	Skirmish at Bridgeport

May 2	Philippi occupied by Confederates	June 19	Skirmish near Petersburg
May 19	Skirmish at Fayetteville	June 26	Skirmish near Springfield
June 14	Martinsburg occupied by Confederates	June 28	Skirmish Sweet Sulphur Springs
June 16	Romney occupied by Confederates	July 3	Skirmish at Darkesville
July 2	Skirmish at Beverly	July 3	Martinsburg occupied by Confederates
July 4	Skirmish at Huttonsville	July 3	Skirmish at North Branch Bridge
July 14	Skirmish at Falling Waters	July 3	Skirmish at North River Mills
July 15	Skirmish near Charlestown	July 4	Skirmish at the North Branch Bridge
July 17	Skirmish at North Mountain	July 4	Battle at Harpers Ferry
July 19	Skirmish near Martinsburg	July 14	Romney occupied by Confederates
August 22	Skirmish near Huttonsville	July 25	Skirmish at Bunker Hill
August 26	Battle of Rocky Gap	July 25	Skirmish at Martinsburg
Sept. 4	Skirmish at Petersburg Gap	July 30	Skirmish at Shepherdstown
Sept. 11	Skirmish near Moorefield	Aug. 4	Skirmish at Keyser
Sept. 15	Skirmish at Smithfield	Aug. 7	Battle of Moorefield
Oct. 13	Battle of Bulltown	Aug. 22	Skirmish at Charlestown
Oct. 18	Attack on Charlestown	Aug. 22	Skirmish at Halltown
Nov. 6	Battle of Droop Mountain	Aug. 29	Skirmish at Charlestown
Nov. 6	Skirmish at Little Sewell Mountain	Sept. 1	Martinsburg occupied by Confederates
Nov. 7	Lewisburg occupied by Federals	Sept. 2	Skirmish at Bunker Hill
Dec. 11	Skirmish at Big Sewell	Sept. 3	Skirmish at Bunker Hill
Dec. 11	Skirmish at Marlin Bottom	Sept. 18	Martinsburg occupied by Confederates
Dec. 12	Lewisburg occupied by Federals	Sept. 27	Skirmish at Buckhannon
Dec. 13	Skirmish at Hurricane Bridge	Sept. 30	Skirmish at Coal R iver
		Oct. 11	Skirmish near Petersburg
		Oct. 26	Skirmish at Winfield

1864

		Oct. 29	Skirmish at Beverly
Jan. 6	Romney occupied by Confederates	Nov. 7	Skirmish at Moorefield
March 3	Skirmish in Grant County	Nov. 27	Skirmish at Moorefield
March 20	Skirmish at the Sinks of Gandy	Nov. 28	Skirmish at Moorefield
April 19	Skirmish at Marlin Bottom	Nov. 28	Skirmish at Keyser
May 3	Skirmish at Bulltown	Nov. 28	Skirmish at Piedmont
May 4	Piedmont captured		
May 6	Skirmish at Princeton		
May 8	Skirmish at Halltown		

1865

May 9	Skirmish on Cheat Mountain		
May 10	Skirmish at Lost River Gap	Jan. 11	Beverly captured
May 11	Romney occupied by Federals	Jan. 15	Skirmish at Petersburg
May 24	Skirmish near Charlestown	March 15	Skirmish at South Fork near Moorefield
June 6	Skirmish at Panther Gap		
June 6	Skirmish at Moorefield	March 22	Skirmish on Patterson Creek, Mineral County
June 10	Skirmish near Kabletown		

Contents

Daguerreotypes.

The subscriber would respectfully inform the citizens of BOONE COUNTY, that he has taken rooms at Boone Court House, where he is prepared to take Daguerreotypes in the most improved style.

He would say to those who wish to get a true and life like picture, that they would do well to call immediately, as his stay is positively short.

Full and complete instructions given and apparatus furnished to those who wish to engage in this beautiful art. Terms reasonable.

JOHN R. WALKER.

Oct. 6th, 1856

John R. Walker was a schoolteacher at the Malden Salt Works in 1850 and a schoolteacher in Shrewsbury in 1860. This ad appeared in the Kanawha Valley Star

CAMP GAULEY BRIDGE,
KANAWHA FALLS, VA. – August 10, 1861

'Mong the mountains of Virginia
Where the waters of Kanawha
Meet the River called New River,
Meet the water called the Gauley,
Where the joyous wedded waters
Dance around a hundred islands,
'Round a hundred rocky islands'
Then the joyous frantic waters
With a voice like roaring thunders
Leap the falls of the Kanawha
Rushing on with headlong fury
Through the gorges wild and rocky
'Mong the mountains grand and hoary,
'Mong nature's time worn castles,
'Mong the mountains adamantine,
And the lofty peaks of granite
In a lone, sequestered valley
Stand the white tents of our army;
Of the army of the Union
Whose reveille wakes the morning,
Wakes the echoes of the mountains,
Wakes to life a slumbering people;
Wakes them by the rolling thunder
By the thunder of its drumming,
By the thunder of its cannon;
By the deep, determined voices
Of its sovereigns and its freemen
Where the shades of Jay and Pinckney,
Where the shades of Clay and Webster
And the shades of Patrick Henry
Stalk at midnight 'mong the mountains,
Startled from their wonted slumbers
By the treason and the traitors,
By the monster of secession
And the danger of the Union.

In a tent of snowy whiteness
Captured from the traitor rebels,
'Mid scenes of death and carnage,
On a storied field of battle,
On the battle field of *"Scary,"*
In this tent of southern cotton'
In this captured tent of cotton
Dwells the soldier *"Arborvitae"*
With his musket and his knapsack,
With his haversack and blanket,
Where he marches with the "Colors"
On Parade or in the *battle:*
Where he gives the men their rations,
Weighs their bread and meat and sugar,
Weighs their coffee, soap and candles'

Where he gives the hungry soldiers
Of the regiment their rations'
Where he serves the host of freedom
With his might and with his valor,
Toiling on and toiling ever,
With a spirit never flagging,
With a *vigilance unceasing,*
And an energy untiring
For his *country* and her *glory;*
Scorning death and scorning danger,
Tasting of fatigue and hunger,
Hoping on and hoping ever
That a life of true devotion
To his country and to freedom,
In the path of *patient duty*
Would help to *work a blessing*
For the weary world of mortals.

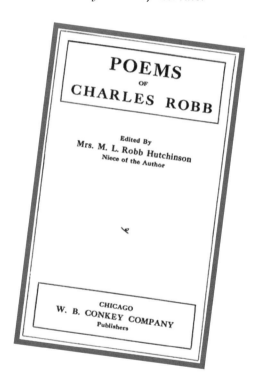

Charles Robb was born January 5, 1826, and during the Civil War was a Commissary Sergeant in Company C, 1st Kentucky Infantry, U.S.A. He passed away September 20, 1872. In 1910 his niece published *Poems of Charles Robb* which included three poems he wrote while in the Gauley Bridge area during the war: "A Legend of the Kanawha," "Arrived at Gauley Bridge, Monday Evening, July 29, 1861," and "Camp Gauley Bridge, Kanawha Falls, Va. – August 10, 1861."

Secession, Restoration,

Statehood

South Carolina and six other Southern states seceded from the Union in the winter of 1860–61 and formed the Confederate States of America. Virginia hoped that the Union could somehow be preserved, but on April 15, 1861, President Lincoln called for troops to put down the rebellion.

Two days later a convention in Richmond passed an ordinance of secession and opted to join the new Confederate States.

People in the western mountainous region of the state had developed a different social and economic life than in the eastern part, and settlements were few. People had to rely on themselves, not slave labor, to produce economic gain.

After the secession ordinance was passed, the western delegates came home, and mass meetings were held throughout the region to denounce the action taken at Richmond. At the First Wheeling Convention on May 13, the foundation for statehood was laid. The Second Wheeling Convention convened on June 11 with 57 delegates attending. A "Restored Government of Virginia" was established with Francis H. Peirpoint as the first governor. The congressmen from the "restored state" were seated in Congress, and President Lincoln recognized them. This secession from another state without that state's permission is unparalleled in American history and has been questioned for constitutionality.

The "Restored Government of Virginia" gave its blessing to the formation of a new state, and the first constitution was completed on February 18, 1862. On April 3, 1862, the Constitution was ratified by a vote of 18,862 to 514 after some changes had been made in the provisions on slavery. On December 31, 1862, President Lincoln signed a bill authorizing the admission of the new state of West Virginia, which was to be called Kanawha. On April 20, 1863, Lincoln issued a proclamation granting statehood, effective June 20, 1863. The capital was established at Wheeling, and Arthur I. Boreman was elected the first governor.

Thirty-nine counties were included in the proposed state after Pocahontas, Greenbrier, Monroe, Mercer and McDowell were added to get more counties with Democratic party majorities. The Republicans did not want any former Virginia slave counties in the state but accepted these five because the mountains in the counties gave the new state a natural barrier. The eastern panhandle counties of Pendleton, Hardy, Hampshire, Berkeley, Jefferson and Morgan were included for protection and because the Baltimore & Ohio Railroad wanted all of its track included in the new state's boundaries.

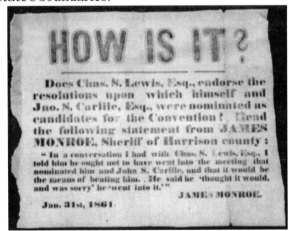

HOW IS IT?

Does Chas. S. Lewis, Esq., endorse the resolutions upon which himself and Jno. S. Carlile, Esq., were nominated as candidates for the Convention? Read the following statement from JAMES MONROE, Sheriff of Harrison county:

" In a conversation I had with Chas. S. Lewis, Esq., I told him he ought not to have went into the meeting that nominated him and John S. Carlile, and that it would be the means of beating him. He said he 'thought it would, and was sorry' he 'went into it.'"

JAMES MONROE.

Jan. 31st, 1861

There will be a public meeting of the citizens of Harrison county, at the court-house in Clarksburg, on court-day, the 14th day of October, 1861: at Good's store, on the 11th: at Sardis, on the 12th: at Shinnston, on the 12th: at Bridgeport, on the 16th: at West Milford, on the 18th: at Romine's Mills, on the 19th: and at Lumberport, on the 19th days of October, 1861, at which the citizens of the county are respectfully requested to be present, when they will be addressed upon the momentous issues involved in the present crisis, and other kindred topics of paramount importance to every freeman and tax payer in the county, by Hon. C. S. Lewis, John J. Davis, Tho. W. Harrison, Caleb Boggess, Tho. L. Moore, and Luther Haymond, or some one or more of them, at the several places above indicated.

October 8th, 1861.

UNION OR DISUNION?

THE ISSUE IS UPON US!

As meetings are being held in portions of our State urging a call for a convention to consider whether Virginia shall unite with South Carolina and the Cotton States in their treasonable efforts to dissolve the Union of these States, it is deemed advisable that the citizens of Harrison county give expression to their sentiments in mass-meeting assembled.

It is the settled conviction of intelligent observers of the times that the Union, formed by our fathers and cemented with their blood---a Union hallowed by all the sacred memories of the past, and endeared to us by the innumerable blessings of the present---is seriously threatened. Even now our monetary interests and business relations have received a shock from the impending destruction of our Government little less disastrous than war itself. The credit of both States and individuals is not only being destroyed, but ruin begins to stare us in the face. Shall Virginia be a participant in this effort at self-destruction? Will she, too, be guilty of self-murder? It is for her People to say. Rely upon it, the time is now come when, if we would avert the horrid calamities of civil war, the people of Harrison should give unmistakable utterance of their devotion to the National Union, and their unalterable attachment and unyielding determination to preserve, unimpaired, the glorious Constitution of the American Confederacy. MARK IT WELL, your silence will be mistaken for indifference, and will tend to strengthen the traitorous hands already stretched forth to destroy the Government. It is of the utmost consequence, then, that the voice of the people be heard, trumpet-tongued, commanding peace. Let every man who values this Government and is opposed to treason, leave his farm, his work-shop, his store, and his counting-room, and give one day to his Country. Do this, we earnestly beseech you, before it is too late. Let no man, therefore, neglect this patriotic call, remembering that he who is not for the Union is against it. Come, then, citizens of Harrison county, to the

MASS-MEETING,

To be held at the Court-house, in Clarksburg, on Saturday next,

The 24th of November, 1860.

Come prepared to resist any and every attempt to sunder the tie which binds us together, and which has hitherto united us as one people.

Clarksburg, Va., November 20th, 1860.

HARPER'S WEEKLY.
A JOURNAL OF CIVILIZATION.

Vol. V.—No. 236.]   NEW YORK, SATURDAY, JULY 6, 1861.   [SINGLE COPIES SIX CENTS.
[$2 50 PER YEAR IN ADVANCE

Entered according to Act of Congress, in the Year 1861, by Harper & Brothers, in the Clerk's Office of the District Court for the Southern District of New York.

CONSTITUENT CONVENTION OF VIRGINIA, ASSEMBLED IN THE CUSTOM HOUSE AT WHEELING, OHIO CO., JUNE, 1861.—SKETCHED BY JASPER GREEN, ESQ.—[SEE NEXT PAGE.]

The Linsly Institute Building in Wheeling was West Virginia's first capitol building. Built in 1858 at the corner of Eoff and Fifteenth streets, its charter dates back to 1814 when it was known as the Lancastrian Academy, the first chartered school for free education in a slave state. The building was used as the capitol from June 20, 1863, to April 1, 1870, in spite of Governor Boreman's repeated requests for a permanent site. Executive offices were again quartered in the building during Wheeling's second capital period from May 23, 1875, to December 4, 1876. The building is still standing but in a modified form.
WEST VIRGINIA STATE ARCHIVES

Custom House at Wheeling, now Independence Hall. FRANK LESLIE'S ILLUSTRATED NEWSPAPER, AUGUST 10, 1861.

Independence Hall in Wheeling, Ohio County, was the site of the birth of West Virginia. It was here in 1861 that the "Declaration of Rights" was adopted and the Restored Government of Virginia was established. The building, erected as a custom house in 1859, is at the corner of Market and Sixteenth streets. It has been restored and is operated by the West Virginia Independence Hall Foundation. In this photo, the building is decked out for the state's 125th anniversary in June 1988.

WEST VIRGINIA STATE ARCHIVES, MICHAEL KELLER PHOTO

TRAITORS IN WHEELING.

Below will be found a complete list of the Traitors and Rebels of Wheeling, Va., who voted May 23, 1861, for the infamous Ordinance of Secession, adopted by the usurpers in the Richmond, Va., Convention.

John Hunter, formerly of Steubenville, Ohio.
Nicholas Crawley, Grocer, Market Square.
J. W. Mitchell, Lawyer.
George Wheller, clerk under John M'Collo. of Co. Court.
Eugene Zane, son of Ebenezar Zane, deceased.
R. A. Stansbury, son of Job Stansbury.
John H. Towers, clerk with Thomas Hughes.
Aaron Kelly, Nail Factory, Benwood.
John Knote, Saddler. Main street.
Edmund P. Zane, Lawyer.
Aber Keyes, clerk with Thomas Hughes.
Dr. Alfred Hughes, brother of Thomas Hughes.
Coorod Goldsborongh.
A. F. Hullihen, Dentist.
T. E. Askew, Confectioner.
James M. Bulger, Coffee House.
Thomas Hughes, Clothing House.
Charles W. Seabright, clerk with T. Hughes.
Rodolph Over.
Wm. Wharton.
Michael Riley, Grocer and Liquors, Market & Monroe sts.
J. B. Riley, clerk with M. Riley.
John W. Orr, shoemaker, from Washington, Pa.
J. Updegraff, Steamboat man.
John Freeze, Steamboat Captain.
J. L. Faunce, from Smithfield, Ohio.
John L. Maxwell, clerk.
Ira Sanger, a New Yorker.
Ebenezer McCoy, botanic doctor.
Walter G. Scott, carpenter.
Wm. Miller, foundry, near creek bridge.
Robert Ibertson, Grocer, corner Market and Union sts.
John Bulger, Saddler.
W. B. Miller, foundry, creek bridge.
John Webb.
Wm. Goudy, sr., carpenter.
James Sweeney, sr., brick maker.
Joseph Caulwell.
William C. Phillips.
Phillip W. Moore, Editor Union.
Tom Strain.

Jerome Pool, coffee house, Washington Hall.
J. H. McNash, formerly of Bosley & McNash.
Thomas M. Riley, (M. Riley's son).
Phil Riley, do do
John L. Bonham, firm of Matthews & Bonham.
James Hanlin, South Wheeling.
Dr. James W. Clemins.
Miles Riley, drayman.
Andrew White, clerk North-Western Bank.
Peter Letcher, Catholic Bookseller, Washington Hall.
Henry Dunlap.
Henry Moore, from Washington, Pa.
George Henry, cigar maker.
Jobe Stansbery, sexton East Wheeling graveyard.
Andy A. Gillespy.
A. M. Phillips, Jr.
Harrison Saylards.
Thos. J. Gardner, lumber merchant, North Wheeling.
H. W. Phillips, Machinist and Foundry, North Wheeilng.
C. W. McKinstry.
A. M. Phillips, Sr.
A. J. Pannell, Lumber Merchant, near Custom House.
W. G. Goshorn.
Alexander Pannell, carpenter.
Daniel Steenrod, Esq.
Hon. Lewis Steenrod.
Wm. P. Wilson, boat builder, firm Wilson, Dunlevy & Co.
John W. Betz.
William Stewart, foundry.
Maddis Ruse,
Dan Dunbar, Engineer.
Wm. McCoy, Cashier of Savings Institute.
Daniel Zane, (Island).
John L. Fry, son of J. L. Fry.
D. J. Dores.
Peter Francis.
S. D. Woodrow.
William Switzer.
William Purcell.
William Otterson, Railroad stone mason.

Apparently not all the citizens of Wheeling sided with the majority of citizens of the western counties.

A GREAT RALLY

OF THE

Friends of Liberty!

TO HELP SAVE THE

BEST GOVERNMENT IN THE WORLD!

WILL BE HELD IN

Fairmont, on Monday, May 6th, Court Day.

Let every man who has the soul, the heart of an American beating within his bosom, be there. The glorious flag of our country has been torn down from the Capitol of our State and the flag of the traitors floats in its place. AMERICANS, we ask you to come to the rescue of our country and our country's cause. Our chains are being forged; their clanking may be heard in Richmond, in that secret, that dark and damnable Convention. Then let all come to the rescue. The great champion of Western Virginia,

HON. JOHN S. CARLILE,

will be there to address the people. Let us give him a warm and glorious reception. Other noble speakers in the cause of our liberties will be there.

FAIRMONT

MAYOR'S PROCLAMATION

MAYOR'S OFFICE,

Wheeling, April 19, 1861.

Whereas apprehensions exist in the minds of many citizens, that violations of the peace of the city may occur in the present excited state of the public mind, upon questions of political import, I deem it advisable to issue this my proclamation, calling upon all good citizens to preserve the public peace and order, at all times, and under all circumstances, and invoking them to refrain from harshness of speech, and from any act which might lead to violence of any kind to any person or property whatsoever, and to render aid to the authorities in maintaining the public peace, protecting property, and in suppressing lawless violence by whomsoever attempted.

A. J. SWEENEY, Mayor.

I do heartily concur in the above proclamation and will use all my official powers to maintain its observance.

EWING, PR.

A. P. WOODS, Chief J. P.

The northern counties of western Virginia were the hotbed of secession from the "traitorous" state of Virginia. The southern and eastern counties bordering eastern Virginia sent a number of their sons to the Southern army.
WEST VIRGINA AND REGIONAL HISTORY COLLECTION

Head Quarters, Virginia Forces,
STAUNTON, VA.

MEN OF VIRGINIA, TO THE RESCUE !

Your soil has been invaded by your Abolition foes, and we call upon you to rally at once, and drive them back. We want Volunteers to march immediately to Grafton and report for duty. Come one ! Come ALL ! and render the service due to your State and Country. Fly to arms, and succour your brave brothers who are now in the field.

The Volunteers from the Counties of Pendleton, Highland, Bath, Alleghany, Monroe, Mercer, and other Counties convenient to that point, will immediately organize, and report at Monterey, in Highland County, where they will join the Companies from the Valley, marching to Grafton.   The Volunteers from the Counties of Hardy, Hampshire, Randolph, Pocahontas, Greenbrier, and other Counties convenient, will in like manner report at Beverly.   And the Volunteers from the Counties of Upshur, Lewis, Barbour, and other Counties, will report at Philippi, in Barbour County.   The Volunteers, as soon as they report at the above points, will be furnished with arms, rations, &c., &c.

Action ! Action ! should be our rallying motto, and the sentiment of Virginia's inspired Orator, "Give me Liberty or give me Death," animate every loyal son of the Old Dominion !   Let us drive back the invading foot of a brutal and desperate foe, or leave a record to posterity that we died bravely defending our homes and firesides,—the honor of our wives and daughters,— and the sacred graves of our ancestors !

[Done by Authority.]
M. G. HARMAN, Maj. Commd'g
at Staunton.
J. M. HECK, Lt. Col. Va. Vol.
R. E. COWAN, Maj. Va. Vol.
May 30, 1861.

Confederate forces in eastern Virginia were not going to give up their western counties without a fight. This led to the Battle of Philippi on June 3, 1861, since called the first land battle of the Civil War.

Headquarters, Va. Forces,

Staunton, June 7th, 1861.

To Arms! To Arms!!
BRAVE MEN
OF THE WEST!!

Drive back the insolent invaders who insult you by their presence on your soil. Our little band of Volunteers have been forced from Phillippa by the *ruthless Northern foe* led on by traitors and tories. It is for you now to rally to the field and **AVENGE THE INSULTED HONOR OF WESTERN VIRGINIA.**

To-day I send to your assistance a force of *Artillery, Cavalry, Infantry* and *Rifles.* To-morrow

AN ARMY WILL FOLLOW

sent to your aid by your patriotic President, JEFFERSON DAVIS, and your noble Governor, JOHN LETCHER.

☞ Arms, Ammunition and Uniforms will be supplied you at your places of rendezvous.

M. G. HARMAN,
Major Commanding.

Notice the spelling of Philippi.

Convention of the People of North Western Virginia

HELD AT WHEELING, MAY 13TH, 1861.

The following RESOLUTIONS were unanimously adopted:

1. *Resolved,* That in our deliberate judgment, the ordinance passed by the Convention of Virginia on the 17th day of April, 1861, known as the ordinance of secession, by which said Convention undertook in the name of the State of Virginia, to repeal the ratification of the Constitution of the United States by this State, and to resume all the rights and powers granted under said Constitution, is unconstitutional, null and void.

2. *Resolved,* That the schedule attached to the ordinance of secession suspending and prohibiting the election of members of Congress for this State, is a manifest usurpation of power, to which we ought not to submit.

3. *Resolved,* That the agreement of the 24th of April, 1861, between the Commissioners of the Confederate States and this State, and the ordinance of the 25th of April, 1861, approving and ratifying said agreement, by which the whole military force and military operations, offensive and defensive, of this Commonwealth, are placed under the chief control and direction of the President of the Confederate States, upon the same principles, basis and footing as if the Commonwealth were now a member of said Confederacy; and all the acts of the executive officers of our State in pursuance of said agreement and ordinance, are plain and palpable violations of the Constitution of the United States, and are utterly subversive of the rights and liberties of the people of Virginia.

4. *Resolved,* That we earnestly urge and entreat the citizens of the State every where, but more especially in the Western section, to be prompt at the polls on the 23d instant; and to impress upon every voter the duty of voting in condemnation of the ordinance of Secession, in the hope that we may not be involved in the ruin to be occasioned by its adoption, and with the view to demonstrate the position of the West on the question of secession.

5. *Resolved,* That we earnestly recommend the citizens of Western Virginia to vote for members of the Congress of the United States, in their several districts, in the exercise of the rights secured to us by the Constitutions of the United States and the State of Virginia.

6. *Resolved,* That we also recommend to the citizens of the several counties to vote at said election for such persons as entertain the opinions expressed in the foregoing resolutions for members of the Senate and House of Delegates of our State.

7. *Resolved,* That in view of the geographical, social, commercial and industrial interests of Northwestern Virginia, this Convention are constrained in giving expression to the opinion of their constituents to declare that the Virginia Convention in assuming to change the relation of the State of Virginia to the Federal Government, have not only acted unwisely and unconstitutionally, but have adopted a policy utterly ruinous to all the material interests of our section, severing all our social ties, and drying up all the channels of our trade and prosperity.

8. *Resolved,* That in the event of the Ordinance of Secession being ratified by a vote, we recommend to the people of the Counties here represented, and all others disposed to co-operate with us, to appoint on the 4th day of June, 1861, delegates to a General Convention, to meet on the 11th of that month, at such place as may be designated by the Committee hereinafter provided, to devise such measures and take such action as the safety and welfare of the people they represent may demand,—each County to appoint a number of Representatives to said Convention equal to double the number to which it will be entitled in the next House of Delegates; and the Senators and Delegates to be elected on the 23d inst., by the counties referred to, to the next General Assembly of Virginia, and who concur in the views of this Convention, to be entitled to seats in the said Convention as members thereof.

9. *Resolved,* That inasmuch as it is a conceded political axiom, that government is founded on the consent of the governed and is instituted for their good, and it cannot be denied that the course pursued by the ruling power in the State, is utterly subversive and destructive of our interests, we believe we may rightfully and successfully appeal to the proper authorities of Virginia, to permit us peacefully and lawfully to separate from the residue of the State, and form ourselves into a government to give effect to the wishes, views and interests of our constituents.

10. *Resolved,* That the public authorities be assured that the people of the North West will exert their utmost power to preserve the peace, which they feel satisfied they can do, until an opportunity is afforded to see if our present difficulties cannot receive a peaceful solution; and we express the earnest hope that no troops of the Confederate States be introduced among us, as we believe it would be eminently calculated to produce civil war.

11. *Resolved,* That in the language of Washington in his letter of the 17th of September, 1787, to the President of Congress: "in all our deliberations on this subject we have kept steadily in view that which appears to us the greatest interest of every true American, the consolidation of our Union, in which is involved our prosperity, felicity, safety and perhaps our national existence." And therefore we will maintain and defend the Constitution of the United States and the laws made in pursuance thereof, and all officers acting thereunder in the lawful discharge of their respective duties.

12. *Resolved,* That John S. Carlile, James S. Wheat, C. D. Hubbard, F. H. Peirpoint, Campbell Tarr, G. R. Latham, Andrew Wilson, S. H. Woodward, and James W. Paxton, be a Central Committee to attend to all the matters connected with the objects of this Convention; and that they have power to assemble this Convention at any time they may think necessary.

13. *Resolved,* That each county represented in this Convention, and any others that may be disposed to co-operate with us, be requested to appoint a Committee of five, whose duty it shall be to correspond with the Central Committee, and to see that all things necessary, be done to carry out the objects of this Convention.

14. *Resolved,* That the Central Committee be instructed to prepare an address to the people of Virginia, in conformity with the foregoing resolutions, and cause the same to be published and circulated as extensively as possible.

By Order of the Convention.

JOHN W. MOSS, PRESIDENT.

G. L. CRANMER,
M. M. DENT, *Secretaries.*
C. B. WAGGENER,

These resolutions at the First Wheeling Convention set the foundation for statehood. This was the first and last time in American history that a portion of a state would break away from the rest of the state without the consent of the entire state's population. WEST VIRGINIA AND REGIONAL HISTORY COLLECTION

CIRCULAR.

HEAD-QUARTERS,
Office of Provost Marshal General, for Virginia.

WHEELING, VA., AUGUST, 23rd, 1862.

1st—Having been appointed Provost Marshal General for State of Virginia by the Secretary of War, I hereby enter upon the duties of the office. The gentlemen whose names are hereto appended are designated Provost Marshals for the Counties named, and will without delay signify their acceptance of the position—this circular being their certificate of appointment. Said officers are charged with the duty of co-operating with the civil and military authorities, in all matters pertaining to the execution of the laws of the Federal and State Governments. They shall make immediate and daily reports to this office of their proceedings.

2nd—Special attention is called to late orders from the War Department, August 8th and August 9th, 1862, entitled respectively: "Order for the suppression of disloyal practices," "Order to prevent the evasion of military duty," "Regulations for Drafting," and to the explanatory circular of Major L. C. Turner, Judge Advocate, August 11th, 1862, printed copies of which are herewith enclosed.

3rd—No citizen shall be arrested upon charges of disloyalty or treasonable practices unless such charges shall be submitted in writing, and the truth of the same attested under oath by the person preferring them. Persons may be arrested when considerable suspicion attaches to their movements, or for other just cause, whereupon instant examination into their cases will be made, and reports forwarded to these Head-Quarters for instructions; those arrested being permitted to furnish good security for their appearance when called for, after taking the prescribed oath of allegiance.

4th—Prisoners will be surrendered to the United States Marshal when they are indicted, and others will, with all papers and information concerning them, be handed over to the Commander of the nearest military Post, when practicable, to be forwarded, if directed, to these Head-Quarters, receipts being taken which will be sent to this office. County and city prisons may be used by Marshals in their discretion, and the keepers thereof are hereby ordered to afford all facilities to carry out this order. Persons arrested, who are charged with having served under the Rebel Government, whether in the Military, Judicial, Executive, or Legislative Departments will not be discharged, but will be committed to the charge of the Commander of the nearest military Post, with sworn statements concerning them, or forwarded to these Head-Quarters, as will be most practicable and economical.

5th—Provost Marshals hereby appointed are authorized to organize such force as may be absolutely indispensable to enable them to execute the orders heretofore specified. They will attest under oath the fact of such necessity, and also the record of necessary expenses, observing the strictest economy in the same, compatible with the public interest. They will make arrests when ordered so to do by the Governor of Virginia, or the Adjutant General of the State, and reports of the same will be sent to either of them, and to this office. They will apply to the Commander of the nearest military Post for any extra force required to execute special orders, or to insure arrests in particular cases, stating the necessity and the authority for the same.

6th.—Attention is called to articles 80, 81, 82, of the Articles of War, (printed copies herewith enclosed,) for government in all matters not hereby specially provided for, relating to the arrest, receipt and discharge of prisoners.

7th.—Provost Marshals will administer the required Oath of Allegiance (copy enclosed,) to all persons who have not previously subscribed to it, and give them certificates that they have taken it.

Aliens will be paroled, not to aid or abet the enemies of the United States, nor to advocate or sustain, either in public or private, the cause of the so-called confederate states, and when deemed necessary, they will be called on to give bond and security for the faithful performance of this obligation. A record of the same will be kept, stating the residence of the parties, which will be sent monthly to this office with the original oaths and paroles.

8th.—All printed forms required by Provost Marshals, in the discharge of their duties, will be promptly furnished from this Office.

PROV. MARSHAL GEN. FOR VA.

PROVOST MARSHAL FOR

Western Virginia was not yet a state of the Union when this circular was posted in August 1862. The Restored Government of Virginia still had jurisdiction in the western counties. WEST VIRGINA AND REGIONAL HISTORY COLLECTION

No. 224.—HON. FRANK H. PIERPONT, ELECTED GOVERNOR OF VIRGINIA BY THE UNION CONVENTION AT WHEELING, IN PLACE OF JOHN LETCHER.

Francis H. Peirpoint (later changed to Pierpont) from Monongalia County was elected governor of the Restored Government of Virginia at the Second Wheeling Convention in June 1861. After the state was admitted to the Union, his government seat was moved to Alexandria, Virginia, and then to Richmond at the end of the war.

A PROCLAMATION.
BY THE GOVERNOR.

In the midst of War and its afflictions, we are more forcibly reminded of our dependence upon Divine Providence ; and, while in all we suffer, we should own His chastening hand, we should be ready to acknowledge that it is of His mercy that we are not destroyed, and that so many of the blessings of life are preserved to us. Seed time and harvest have not failed ; the early and the latter rain have fallen in their seasons, and the toil of the husbandman has been abundantly repaid. It is, therefore, becoming that while we earnestly pray that the days of our affliction may be shortened, we should thankfully acknowledge the manifold mercies, of which, nationally and individually, we are still the recipients.

Now, therefore, I, FRANCIS H. PEIRPOINT, Governor of Virginia, do hereby recommend to the good people of the Commonwealth, the observance of THURSDAY, THE 28TH INST., as a day of Thanksgiving to Almighty God for the blessings of the year ; and of humble and fervent prayer that He will, in more abundant mercy, bring to a speedy end the heart-burnings and civil strife, which are now desolating our country, and restore to our Union its ancient foundations of brotherly love and just appreciation. And I do further recommend that all secular business and pursuits, be, as far as possible, suspended on that day.

IN TESTIMONY WHEREOF, I have hereunto set my hand, and caused the Great Seal of the Commonwealth to be affixed, at the City of Wheeling, this 14th day of November, in the year of our Lord, one thousand eight hundred and sixty-one, and of the Commonwealth, the eighty-sixth.

L. S.

FRANCIS H. PEIRPOINT.

By the Governor :

L. A. HAGANS, Sec'y Commonwealth.

BY THE GOVERNOR OF WEST VIRGINIA.

A PROCLAMATION.

Whereas, it is made known to me, Arthur I. Boreman, Governor of the State of West Virginia, that evil-disposed and seditious persons in the county of Jefferson are endeavoring to incite the people of that county to a resistance and violation of the constitution and laws of West Virginia by maintaining that said County is not legally and constitutionally a part of said State, and therefore they are not bound to obey its authority; and by openly endeavoring to persuade and induce the people of said County to hold an election therein for a Member of Congress, and for a Senator and Delegates to the General Assembly of Virginia under the assumed authority of the State of Virginia, thereby attempting to set up and establish in said County a government and jurisdiction, other, different and separate from that of the State of West Virginia, all of which is not only in defiance of the regularly constituted authorities, but must result, if persisted in, in great disturbance of the peace and good order of society.

In order that the people of Jefferson County may not be misled and unwittingly induced to violate the law, I state that the actions and conduct of the evil disposed and seditious persons above mentioned are not approved, or even countenanced by the Executive of Virginia, but are in direct opposition to his advice and counsel to the contrary.

Civil organization has been restored and maintained in the county of Jefferson under the authority solely of the State of West Virginia, without any pretence of jurisdiction by the authorities of Virginia, and it must be apparent to all that the Executive of West Virginia cannot for a moment allow wicked men who are regardless of the peace of the community, to oppose the execution of the laws of the State, or to attempt to set up a different and antagonistic authority therein.

If there is really any *bona fide* doubt as to whether the county of Jefferson is legally and constitutionally a part of West Virginia, or still remains a part of Virginia, that is a question which can be settled in a peaceful and orderly mode, and it seems to me that all persons who have respect for law and have the good of society at heart, will pursue this mode, and will not endeavor to inflame the passions of the people and induce them to attempt the redress of supposed grievances by force or violence.

But I am induced to believe that the leading spirits in this movement in the county of Jefferson are those who left their homes and went South and engaged in the effort to destroy the government and disintegrate the Union, and having been defeated and disappointed in their efforts to accomplish this wicked purpose, they have been allowed, through the benignity of that government, to return with the understanding that they would be peaceable and useful citizens; but instead of keeping faith with the authorities and counselling respect and observance of the laws, they are putting forth all their energies and efforts to disturb, distract and produce discontent amongst the people of their county who otherwise would enjoy peace, good order, contentment and happiness.

In order therefore that the proper authority may be maintained and the peace of the community preserved, I, Arthur I. Boreman, Governor as aforesaid, do, by this my proclamation, counsel, advise, and warn the people of Jefferson County, and all others, against any further resistance or opposition to, or violation of, the constitution and laws of West Virginia, and especially against any attempt to hold an election under the assumed authority of the State of Virginia, or any authority other than that of West Virginia; and make known that, if such attempt is persisted in, the parties engaged therein will be arrested and brought to punishment. And I hereby direct all civil officers in said County to arrest and bring to justice every person who attempts to hold an election in said County, under the assumed authority of the State of Virginia, or any authority other than that of the State of West Virginia; and the military authorities of the United States in the District of West Virginia are called on and requested to issue such orders, and to use such force as may be deemed necessary to prevent such election being held, and, if attempted, to aid the civil authorities in arresting the parties engaged therein, and in bringing them to justice.

In Testimony Whereof, I have hereunto set my hand and caused the seal of the said State to be affixed at the Capitol in { SEAL. } the City of Wheeling, this 9th day of October in the year of Our Lord eighteen hundred and sixty-five, and of the State the third.

ARTHUR I. BOREMAN.

BY THE GOVERNOR:

GRANVILLE D. HALL,
Secretary of the State.

Arthur I. Boreman of Tyler County was elected first governor of the new state. He presided over the Second Wheeling Convention in June 1861. The three eastern counties of Morgan, Berkeley and Jefferson felt more kinship with their eastern brothers than the new state of West Virginia. They were included in the new state to give protection to the vital Baltimore & Ohio Railroad which passed through the counties.

WEST VIRGINIA AND REGIONAL HISTORY COLLECTION

LINCOLN

SEWARD

By the President of the United States of America.

A Proclamation.

Whereas, by the Act of Congress approved the 31st day of December, last, the State of West Virginia was declared to be one of the United States of America, and was admitted into the Union on an equal footing with the original States in all respects whatever, upon the condition that certain changes should be duly made in the proposed Constitution for that State;

And, whereas, proof of a compliance with that condition as required by the Second Section of the Act aforesaid, has been submitted to me;

Now, therefore, be it known, that I Abraham Lincoln, President of the United States, do, hereby, in pursuance of the Act of Congress aforesaid, declare and proclaim that the said act shall take effect and be in force, from and after sixty days from the date hereof.

In witness whereof, I have hereunto set my hand and caused the Seal of the United States to be affixed.

Done at the city of Washington, this twentieth day of April, in the year of our Lord one thousand eight hundred and sixty-three, and of the Independence of the United States the eighty-seventh.

Abraham Lincoln

By the President:

William H. Seward,
Secretary of State.

The statehood proclamation signed by President Lincoln on April 20, 1863, established the state of West Virginia, effective 60 days hence, June 20, 1863. This brought to conclusion the statehood process of two years' duration in Wheeling. Wheeling was the most political, transportation, industrial, retail and social center in the new state in the latter half of the nineteenth century. It was twice the capital of the state.

THE NEW STATE.

The Counties Comprising the New Commonwealth of West Virginia, the Thirty-Fifth State of the Union.

Notice that the eastern panhandle counties of Berkeley and Jefferson are missing from this map.

FRANK LESLIE'S ILLUSTRATED NEWSPAPER.
FRANK LESLIE, Editor and Publisher.

NEW YORK, SEPTEMBER 7, 1861.

All Communications, Books for Review; &c., must be addressed to FRANK LESLIE, 19 City Hall Square, New York.

TERMS FOR THIS PAPER.

One Copy......................	17 weeks	$ 1
One do.	1 year	
Two do.	1 year	$ 5
Or One Copy	2 years	$ 5
Three Copies	1 year	$ 8
Five do.	1 year (to one address)	$10

And an extra Copy to the person sending a Club of Five. Every additional subscription, $2.

The State of Kanawha.

CONTRARY to the best judgment of most, but in consonance with the wishes of many, the Western Virginia State Convention, by a vote of 50 to 28, passed an ordinance on the 20th of August, subject, however, to popular ratification, establishing 39 of the western counties of Virginia as an independent commonwealth, to be known as the State of Kanawha. These counties, all of which were represented in the Convention, lie to the westward of the main chain of the Alleghanies, embracing that anomalous district projecting up between the Ohio River and Pennsylvania, and known as the "Pan Handle," and extending downward to about latitude 37 deg. 20 min. Only unmistakable Union counties are embraced in the new State, although provision is made in the ordinance for receiving such other counties as may vote to be included. It should be premised that for various reasons, one of which was the exclusion of slaves under a certain age from taxation, free Western Virginia has several times attempted to sever her connection from Eastern or slaveholding Virginia. Once, if we mistake not, an act for separation came within one vote of being carried—John Letcher, the present rebel Governor of Virginia, supporting the measure.

The motives for separation, therefore, have not arisen altogether from present complications. They have nevertheless been patent and conclusive, viewed from the Western Virginian standpoint. In the first place, the counties composing the new State embrace a rich lumber, mineral and grazing district, in parts well adapted for the cultivation of cereals. It nowhere produces the tropical or semi-tropical staples, for the successful cultivation of which servile labor is deemed requisite. The 39 counties composing the new State have a total population, according to the census of 1860, of 281,786 souls, of which less than 8,000 are slaves. The country is therefore, practically, a free country, and as such opposed to the Secession heresy. The total population of Virginia, under the census referred to, was 1,593,199, including 495,826 slaves, leaving a white population of 1,097,373. So that in losing the population of the new State, amounting to 281,986, Virginia is shorn of about one-fourth of her white inhabitants. It is well known that there are at least 20 other counties, embracing nearly the whole of Middle Virginia, or the valley of Virginia, which would attach themselves to the new State if circumstances enabled them to give a free expression of opinion. Indeed, more than half of Virginia is regarded as "Union" against "Secession." As it now stands organized (and in recognizing the new State we bow to the necessities of the case), the new commonwealth of Kanawha is one of the richest in resources of the whole Union, and in the decade between 1850 and 1860 increased more rapidly in population and wealth than any other equal extent of territory in the slave States. It abounds in minerals, coal, iron, salt and mineral oil, and with its agricultural resources possesses all the natural elements of wealth, besides the inestimable blessing of free labor. It cannot fail to become rich and powerful. It is, moreover, a region of rivers and mountains, amongst which Liberty loves to dwell, and where the strong right arms of men hew out the pillars which support the temple of Freedom.

The wisdom of the present movement, in a technical, perhaps in a political sense, fails to commend itself to the popular judgment. It, in some sort, recognises the right of Secession, which the Government of the United States, anxious to conserve the forms of legality, rigidly denies. That Government at once accepted Governor Pierpont as the *de facto* and *de jure* Governor of Virginia, in place of John Letcher, on the ground that the latter had undertaken to perform acts not sanctioned by the letter or spirit of the Constitution and laws of the State, and had forfeited, in consequence, any claim on the loyalty of the commonwealth. It is no doubt sound policy in the Federal Government thus to recognize the action of the loyal men in the several States, as the nucleus for their reorganization. It is easy to see how every State, with the possible exception of South Carolina, might thus regularly, and with all the sanction of form, be brought back into the Union. With the advance of the Federal arms, the present suppressed Union sentiment in every State might find safe expression—all that is requisite to prove that Secession and its attendant ills are the work of conspirators, and of a traitorous minority.

The action of the State Convention of Virginia, therefore, cannot fail to be embarrassing to the programme of the Government for restoring the Union. But the results achieved are nevertheless such as would have followed on any plan of reorganizing the country. Neither in sympathy nor interest is Western Virginia allied to Eastern Virginia. The social organization of its people, their interests and sentiments, are different and irreconcilable, and a separation now only anticipates a result sure to follow in the course of time, and which probably the present is the best time for bringing about. The legal adviser of the Government, the Attorney-General, pronounces against the action of the Convention as "an original, independent act of revolution," and advises an adherence to legal formulas "as dictated by the plainest teachings of prudence." But the political Saurians who compose the *personnel* of the actual Government do not recognize the fact that we are in a state of revolution, earnest, downright and vital, involving not only the national integrity, but every principle of popular government, and that mere formulas will not save us. We must recognize, as the Wheeling Convention has done, the inexorable logic of facts. The Legislature assembled at Wheeling we had admitted to be the Legislature of Virginia—at any rate we have accepted United States Senators chosen by it as Senators of the United States duly elected. If that Legislature, therefore, approves the act of the Convention, and it is afterwards approved by Congress (and of the approval of both bodies there can be no doubt), then all the requirements of the Constitution as to the division and admission of States will be fulfilled. We welcome the State of Kanawha into the national galaxy! May her star be "fixed" and its light steady.

Those of our readers who are statistically inclined will find material for preservation in the following table, showing the population by counties (according to the census of 1860), of this new State of Kanawha:

County	Pop.	County	Pop.
Logan county	4,538	Barbour	8,958
Wyoming	2,865	Upshur	7,292
Raleigh	3,367	Harrison	13,790
Fayette	5,997	Lewis	7,999
Nicholas	4,626	Braxton	4,992
Webster	1,555	Clay	1,787
Randolph	4,990	Kanawha	14,575
Tucker	1,428	Boone	4,840
Preston	13,312	Wayne	6,747
Monongalia	13,048	Cabell	8,020
Marion	12,721	Putnam	6,301
Taylor	7,463	Mason	9,155
Jackson	8,306	Wood	11,046
Roanoke	8,048	Pleasants	2,945
Calhoun	3,502	Tyler	6,517
Wirt	3,751	Doddridge	5,203
Gilmer	3,759	Wetzel	6,703
Ritchie	6,847	Marshall	13,001
Ohio	22,422	Hancock	4,445
Brooke	5,494		
Total population			281,786

Civil War Photographs

Photography in the West Virginia campaigns, excepting Harpers Ferry and parts of the eastern panhandle, was an uncommon occupation. The rugged terrain made it difficult to transport the heavy, cumbersome photographic paraphernalia of the day, and campaigns were usually short and engagements small. Additionally, much of the activity involved guerilla warfare and raids, neither conducive to photographic opportunities.

Despite these shortcomings, there were a small number of photographic images taken within West Virginia during the war. Less than 50 photographic images have been located (excepting portraits and the eastern panhandle), and sadly the identity of most of the photographers has been lost to time. A surprising number of images taken in the vicinity of Gauley Bridge in Fayette County have recently been discovered, and most are believed to have been taken in April 1862. The photographer is unknown, but a likely candidate may be Dr. Claudius Mathieu Pitrat of Buffalo, Putnam County, who had the equipment and means.

There were four primary forms of photography during the war: daguerreotype, the ambrotype, the tintype, and the carte-de-visite. The daguerreotype, one of the first photographic processes, was invented around 1839 by Louis J.M. Daguerre (1789–1851). The process used silver or copper-coated metallic plates, sensitive to light, which were developed by mercury vapor. The image is as if looking in a mirror, therefore the view is reversed. Daguerreotypes were more expensive than ambrotypes or tintypes and were less sought by the common soldier.

Ambrotypes were invented in 1854 by James Ambrose Cutting (1814–1867) of Boston, and his partner Isaac Rehn of Philadelphia. This process involved a thin photographic glass negative made to serve as a positive picture.

Tintypes, or melainotypes or ferrotypes, involved a process of making "photographic pictures on japanned surfaces" such as iron. The first U.S. patent for this process was issued February 19, 1856, to Professor Hamilton L. Smith of Kenyon College in Ohio.

Carte-de-visites were a very popular form of paper portraits and were used primarily as visiting cards, or name cards with photos. These were first mentioned in the United States in 1858, and thousands were issued during the war, attesting to their popularity.

Stereoscopic views and battlefield photographs were also popular with the home folks during the war, but as with many of the above types of photography, the men behind the cameras may never be known.

The actual daguerreotype camera owned by Dr. Claudius Pitrat of Buffalo, West Virginia.
BILL WINTZ COLLECTION

Carte-De-Visite

One of the most popular forms of photography during the war was the *carte–de–visite*, or visiting card, a form of paper portrait. Andre Adolphe Disderi introduced the *carte–de–visite* (c.d.v.) in 1854, and it received its name from the Duke of Parma, who in 1857, requested his photographer produce a more conveniently sized photo, such as the size of a calling card. Hence the name *carte–de–visite*, which translates roughly as calling or visiting card. It is believed these first appeared in the U.S. at the 1858 Exhibition at the Franklin Institute in Philadelphia. This type of imagery, in which the individual's photo, as opposed to their printed name, exploded with popularity between 1860 and 1866, and in 1861 Edward Anthony of New York produced an album for storing and preserving *carte-de-visites* in the home.

Nearly every state had numerous carte-de-visite photographers, and West Virginia was no exception. Many of their names have been lost with the passing of time. Some of the more prominent ones known in West Virginia by surviving *carte-de-visites* and their photographic gallery backmarks include:

Asa C. Partridge of Wheeling, Ohio County, was born circa 1820 in Vermont. He first appeared at Wheeling in the 1850 census as a "portrait maker" and in the 1860 census as an "artist." On October 17, 1852, Partridge married Elizabeth A. Filbricke [Fellbrick] and in 1856 went into a photography partnership with T.H. Higgins, which lasted four years. Higgins, born in Ohio County in 1838, was schooled at Wheeling and developed an interest in photography at an early age. After leaving his photography partnership with Partridge, he went into business for himself and was considered Wheeling's premier photographer until retiring in 1898. Partridge, however, is the most prominent name found on backmarks during the war period.

Another photographer in Wheeling during the war was 23-year-old John Brown, apparently no relation to the famous abolitionist.

In Parkersburg could be found Charles Amos Wade. He was born in Bath County, Virginia, April 30, 1836, the son of Leonard Cassell Wade and Sarah Matheny. He moved with his parents to Wood County, (West) Virginia where he spent most of his life. He was a photographer and druggist, and appears as a 23-year-old photographer in the 1860 census. Wade was active in politics as a Democrat, and in 1876 was elected sheriff of Wood County. He was a member of the Methodist Episcopal Church. He married Isabella MacNeil on November 9, 1864. Wade died June 11, 1908.

J. Frank Miller was a photographer on Main Street in Clarksburg, Harrison County. No information has been located on him.

In Charleston, Kanawha County, the most prominent backmark is that of the photographic gallery of Hover & Stahl, possibly photographers from Ohio. They took many military and civilian portraits in Charleston, probably in 1863 or 1864, and numerous images were of Ohio soldiers.

Another photographic gallery in Charleston was that of Godley & Gates. Their identities are not known, but Gates may have been Alexander Gates, a photographer in his late teens believed to have been a resident of the Point Pleasant, Mason County, area or Gallipolis, Ohio, during the war. He appears in the 1870 census as a 28-year-old photographer in Charleston.

Other West Virginia backmarks in existence include Martinsburg and Harpers Ferry, and certainly there must have been others.

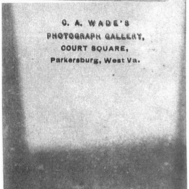

C. A. WADE'S
PHOTOGRAPH GALLERY,
COURT SQUARE,
Parkersburg, West Va.

Hover & Stahl's
Photograph
GALLERY.
Charleston, W. Va.

Photographed by
J. FRANK MILLER,
Main Street,
Clarksburgh, West Va.

N. B. Negative never destroyed. Duplicates to be had at any time.

No............

GODLEY & GATES
Photograph
GALLERY,
Charleston, VA.

Three unidentified Carte-de-Visites:. The right image shows a "VA"—possibly for [West] Virginia—on the soldier's hat.

LEFT AND MIDDLE:
RICHARD ANDRE COLLECTION
RIGHT: TERRY LOWRY COLLECTION

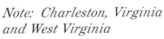

Note: Charleston, Virginia and West Virginia

JOHN BROWN, Wheeling, West Va.

Private William Doran, 2nd West Virginia Cavalry Note: Photographer John Brown of Wheeling, West Va.
L.M. STRAYER COLLECTION

E.C. Thomas, Surgeon, 3rd Regiment [West] Virginia Volunteer Mounted Infantry.
RONNIE ANN TRONT COLLECTION

Union volunteers assembled at the corner of High and Walnut streets in Morgantown, Monongalia County, in 1861. Unit designation is unknown.
PICTORIAL HISTORIES
COLLECTION

German Street looking east in Shepherdstown, Jefferson County in 1861. The Trinity Episcopal Church was built in the 1850s. This is the oldest photograph in the collection of the Jefferson County Museum. Shepherdstown, the oldest community in the state, saw the passing of both armies through the area, especially before and after the nearby battle at Sharpsburg, Maryland, in 1862. JEFFERSON COUNTY MUSEUM

Bennett Dowler Rider

Bennett D. Rider, a prominent photographer of Clarksburg and Harrison County during the war, as well as later, was born January 9, 1833, in Harrison County, (West) Virginia, the son of John W. and Sarah Bird.

The 1840 census lists the family as living in Harrison County, but in the 1850 census they are listed in Upshur County. Sometime during the 1850s they returned to Harrison County where Bennet D. Rider married Hester J. Williams, April 18, 1859. He was a resident of Sycamore Dale where he taught school briefly, served as a merchant and miller, and became the first postmaster at Sycamore Dale. Rider died October 12, 1890, at West Milford, Harrison County, and laid to rest at Sycamore Cemetery. His widow Hester moved to Buckhannon, Upshur County, where she died January 2, 1939, one year shy of a hundred years of age.

Rider and his studio.

These two soldiers's portraits were taken by Rider in Clarksburg during the war. The soldier on the right belonged to the 17th Corps, U.S. Army.
ALL PHOTOS WEST VIRGINIA STATE ARCHIVES

This rare photo taken by Bennett Rider in 1863 shows Main Street looking east between Third and Fourth streets in Clarksburg, Harrison County. Clarksburg, the county seat got its name at a meeting of settlers sometime between 1778 and 1781. During the war the town was a supply depot for the Union army and the birthplace of Confederate General Thomas J. "Stonewall" Jackson. HARRISON COUNTY HISTORICAL SOCIETY

This image of the steamboat Silver Lake No. 2 *was taken at Vicksburg "after the fall" of the town, July 4, 1863. Built in Wellsville, Ohio, in 1861 and sold to the U.S. Army, she brought troops and supplies up the Kanawha River to Charleston in May 1863. The* Kanawha Republican *wrote, "There came up the Kanawha, on Saturday last to our place, a formidable looking craft, clad in iron mail. Her guns, we should think, would do admirable execution against an enemy, at a pretty long distance. Capt. Rodgers, his officers and men, by their gentlemanly deportment and fighting spirit, have won the highest regard of our people." The boat's name was changed to* Marion *in 1865 and a year later she sank in far-off Montana.*

MILLER'S *PHOTOGRAPHIC HISTORY OF THE CIVIL WAR.*

Mustering in of officers of the 6th West Virginia Cavalry. Photographer and location unknown.

STEVE CUNNINGHAM COLLECTION

A long distance view of Charles Town (Charlestown at that time) during the war. This small community, the county seat of Jefferson County was also the scene of much action before the war (John Brown's trial) and all through the war.

HARPERS FERRY NATIONAL HISTORICAL PARK HF-13

Photographers

Dr. Claudius Mathieu Pitrat was born in Lyon, France, on April 5, 1811. He came to the United States in 1839, settling in Buffalo, Putnam County, in 1840. In the early 1850s he built a three-story steam flour mill at Buffalo and was also involved in the Buffalo Academy. He owned a general store and served as postmaster of the community. Pitrat was also known as an amateur photographer, taking many daguerreotype photos of area scenes and steamboats. In the July 1858 issue of the *The Wreath of the Kanawha*, a bi-monthly publication by the students of the Buffalo Academy, the following ad ran:

If you wish to have a picture taken, call on Dr. Pitrat and he will give you one so handsome, if not more so, then the original. The Dr. is a scientific artist, and not a run-about-humbug. He studies to please and pleases to study.

His brother Julies Etienne Pitrat became famous for inventing the computing scale and due to his northern sentiment, moved from Buffalo to Gallipolis, Ohio, during the war. Dr. Pitrat died at Buffalo on Dec. 25, 1891, and is buried in the Mound City Cemetery at Gallipolis.

A Frenchman by the name of **Favre** was also a photographer in the Kanawha Valley. In her memoirs, Mollie Hansford of Coalsmouth (St. Albans) recalled three Frenchmen coming to Coalsmouth; one taught French, one dancing and one was an artist and took daguerrotypes, the first that were ever seen here.

Unidentified Union officer's photograph, taken by Briant's Photographic Gallery, Market Street, north of the courthouse, Parkersburg. Briant was probably Alfred Bryant, a 28-year-old artist listed in the 1860 Wood County census. MATHENY'S WOOD COUNTY IN THE CIVIL WAR

The second bridge over the Gauley River at Gauley Bridge, Fayette County. It was built in February 1862 to replace the old covered bridge at the same location that was burned by Confederate troops in late July 1861. This bridge was destroyed by Union troops in September 1862 on their retreat from Gen. W.W. Loring's troops down the Kanawha River to Charleston. It was not until 1926 that a new bridge was built across the river. Piers from this bridge can still be seen.
TIM McKINNEY COLLECTION

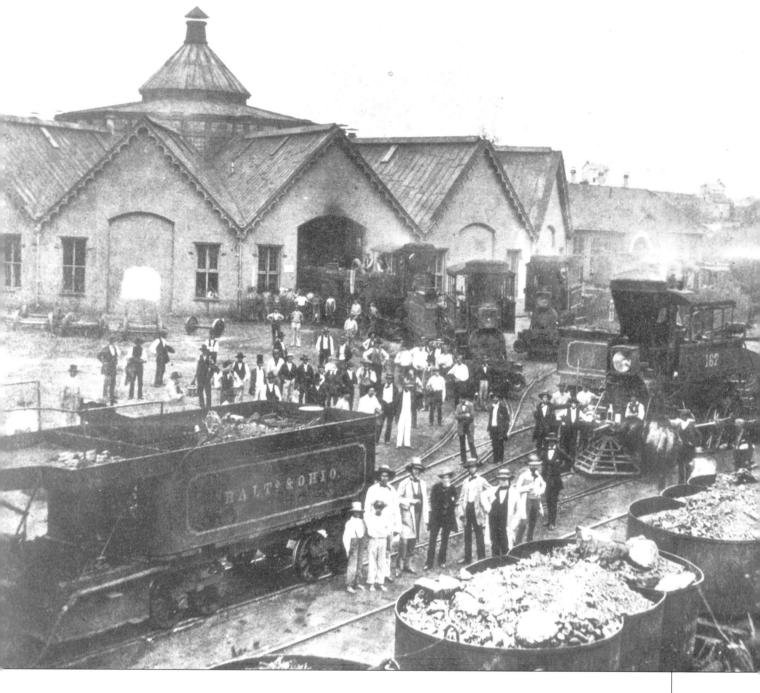

Above: This remarkable view at the Baltimore & Ohio Railroad roundhouse in Martinsburg, Berkeley County, was taken in either 1858 or 1860. It shows the yards packed with "Camels." These engines were designed by Ross Winans of the B&O. They were the first coal-burning locomotives to be produced in large numbers. Nearly 300 were built, and some ran for more than 40 years. The cab was placed atop the boiler to reduce the weight of the firebox. The circular tubs in the foreground are loaded with coal bound for Baltimore.

Top right: A Winans eight-wheel "Camel" locomotive at Martinsburg in 1860.

Bottom right: The hotel and train station in Grafton, Taylor County, in 1860. The B&O mainline is on the right, the Northwestern branchline on the left. The Northwestern Railroad from Grafton to Parkersburg, was finished in 1857. The tracks of the two lines carried the troops and supplies for the eastern and western theaters of war. The railroad was the cause of frequent battles, raids and skirmishes throughout the war, and its protection tied up thousands of Union troops all along the line.

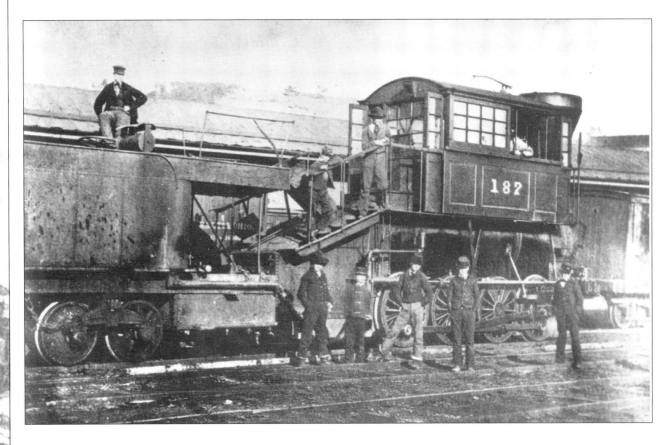

This series of 13 (or more) images was taken in Fayette County in the area between Kanawha Falls and Hawks Nest. Three of the images were later drawn in sketch form by artist Harry Fenn to accompany Gen. Jacob D. Cox's article "McClellan In West Virginia" which ran in The Century *magazine in the mid-1880s and later in the book* Battles and Leaders of the Civil War. *Date and photographer are unknown, but it is believed they were taken in April 1862 and possibly by the same photographer of the outdoor images of the 28th, 34th and 47th Ohio infantry regiments. A possible photographer is Dr. Claudius Mathieu Pitrat of Buffalo, Putnam County, who photographed the 7th West Virginia Cavalry at Buffalo in 1862. He had the equipment and the means, and the time frame is correct, yet this is only speculation. Most of these images recently were located at the West Virginia State Archives but were incorrectly dated in the mid-1880s, the time of the* Century *magazine articles. Civil War historian Tim McKinney discovered this discrepancy and also located some of the images in the personal collection of the late Aubrey Musick of Gauley Bridge. The collection at the State Archives is noted as the Forbes Collection. Years later the* Fayette Tribune *claimed a soldier named Goldsticker took these photos, but this has never been verified.*

The second bridge across the Gauley River as shown on page 25.

The rear of what may be the Miller home in Gauley Bridge can be seen in the middle background behind the barn. This home still stands. The 1862 suspension bridge is to the left. Cotton Hill is in the left background.

Picket post on a rock near Gauley Bridge. They are carrying artillery pattern Enfield rifles and sabers, indicating cavalry. They may be members of the 2nd West Virginia Cavalry, which was in the area at the time.

Top: View of Kanawha Falls showing a mill on the south side of the Kanawha River.

Bottom left: View of Kanawha Falls showing the post hospital and the wagon shop.

Bottom right: View of Kanawha Falls showing the post hospital and the wagon shop.

When placed side to side, these three images present an excellent panoramic view of Kanawha Falls.

Top and bottom left: View from Hawks Nest.

Bottom right: View between Tompkins farm and Gauley Bridge.

Top: Gauley Mount and Tompkins farm, home of Col. Christopher Q. Tompkins, 22nd Virginia Infantry, CSA, and used as a camp by Federal soldiers.

Bottom left: Road to Tompkins farm after crossing the bridge. Gauley Bridge camps can be seen in left corner at the bridge.

Bottom right: View between Tompkins farm and Gauley Bridge.

Hawks Nest looking east and the community of Gauley Bridge, Fayette County. These images were probably taken by the same unknown photographer who took the previous images.
AUBREY MUSICK COLLECTION

Field and staff of the 47th Ohio Volunteer Infantry taken at Tompkins farm near Gauley Bridge in April 1862. Based upon the time frame and uniform rank designations, the men are possibly identified as: standing, left to right—Surgeon George (Charles) A. Spies or Stephen P. Bonner, Col. Frederick Poschner, Lt. Col. Augustus C. Parry or Lyman S. Elliott, Adjutant John G. Durbeck or George M. Ziegler, and Assistant Surgeon Augustus Hoeltze. The man seated in front is either a captain or a lieutenant.

First lieutenants and officers of the 47th Ohio Volunteer Infantry taken in April 1862 at Tompkins farm near Gauley Bridge, Fayette County. Several officers were apparently absent when this photo was taken. LARRY M. STRAYER COLLECTION

Extremely rare outdoor photo of the sergeants of Company A, 34th Ohio Volunteer Infantry (Piatt's Zouaves) taken at the Tompkins farm near Gauley Bridge, in the Spring of 1862. Left to right: 1st Sgt. B.J. Ricker (later Major, 36th Ohio Volunteer Infantry), unknown, Andrew Temple, C.P. Bennett, unknown. LARRY M. STRAYER COLLECTION

Col. Augustus Moor of the 28th Ohio Volunteer Infantry.
MASSACHUSETTS COMMANDERY, MILITARY ORDER OF THE LOYAL LEGION AND THE U.S. ARMY MILITARY HISTORY INSTITUTE

Regimental band of the 28th Ohio Volunteer Infantry, 1862, winter quarters, Gauley Bridge. The soldier in the far left foreground appears to be Col. Augustus Moor.
KJYSTEN W. DREW COLLECTION

A rare photographic view titled "Headquarters – 28th Ohio Vol-Gauley Bridge, W.Va." This is one of only two known views of the 28th in the field. The officer in the middle front with his right hand inside his coat appears to be Col. Augustus Moor of the 28th. The other soldiers are probably members of his staff. The photo was probably taken in April 1862. This image was found on a small silver picture ornament to the left, probably given to veterans of the regiment after the war.

Regimental mess of the 23rd Ohio Volunteer Infantry near Beckley, Raleigh County. Col. Rutherford B. Hayes is on the far left. (top photo). Colonel Hayes, center background, witnessing a friendly sabre bout (bottom photo). Although these two images are often attributed to a Jan. 24, 1862 date, that would not be possible as the 23rd Ohio was yet stationed at Fayetteville, Fayette County, on that date. A more likely date would be sometime in March or April 1862 when the regiment was at Beckley. Colonel Hayes went on to a distinguished career and was elected President of the United States in 1877. William McKinley also served in this regiment and was elected President of the United States in 1897.

RUTHERFORD B. HAYES LIBRARY - #503 & 553

Carte-de-visite of Billy Crump, Company I, 23rd Ohio Volunteer Infantry, and an orderly to Colonel Hayes when he was stationed at Camp Reynolds near Gauley Bridge, in February 1863. Below he is shown at Camp Reynolds on Hayes' horse, which he borrowed, along with his pistol. He set off from camp and traveled 20 miles to forage for supplies.
RUTHERFORD B. HAYES LIBRARY
U.S. ARMY MILITARY HISTORY INSTITUTE

Camp Reynolds, the 1862–63 winter quarters of the 23rd Ohio Volunteer Infantry at Kanawha Falls, Fayette County. Originally called Camp Maskell, the name was changed to Camp Reynolds in honor of Maj. Eugene E. Reynolds who was killed at the battle of South Mountain, Maryland. This is undoubtedly the photo mentioned by Col. Rutherford B. Hayes of the 23rd Ohio in a letter written to his uncle from Camp White, (Charleston) on April 9, 1863, which reads, "I send you a soldier's photograph of our log cabin camp near Gauley. It is not good. You can see the falls beyond the camp and the high cliffs on the opposite side of the Kanawha [River]. My quarters were at the long-roofed cabin running across the street towards the back and right of the picture." Although the photographer is unknown, it may well have been a member of the 23rd Ohio, as Hayes wrote his wife on April 5, 1863, "Enclosed photographs [probably all portraits], except Comly's, are taken by a Company B man who is turning a number of honest pennies by the means—Charlie Smith . . . Captain Avery's orderly." RUTHERFORD B. HAYES LIBRARY

*Left: Major Eugene Reynolds
Below: Capt. Avery's orderly
Charlie Smith who photographed scenes and people in
Camp Reynolds.*

Union troops, believed to be the 12th West Virginia Infantry, at Camp Wiley (also known as Carlisle) on Wheeling Island, 1862.
WHEELING AREA HISTORICAL SOCIETY VIA ELLEN DUNABLE

In the early part of the war the Wheeling or Rosecrans ambulance was fashioned after a design by General W.S. Rosecrans and manufactured by the Wheeling Wagon and Carriage Company. It was drawn by two horses and could handle eleven or twelve men sitting or two recumbent and three sitting. Hundreds of ambulances were shipped out of Wheeling, and it was also used in the city to transport the sick and wounded to the hospital. This photo was possibly taken in Wheeling or Cincinnati, Ohio.
WHEELING HOSPITAL ARCHIVES VIA MARGARET BRENNAN

George W Parsons, the photographer credited with the photos of the Ringgold Cavalry at New Creek (Keyser) in Mineral County, is probably the same George W. Parsons born in Randolph County, November 15, 1838, the son of Jonathan Parsons and Mary Neville. The family yet remained in Randolph County in 1850, and when the war broke out, Parsons was appointed train master in the Federal army, a position he held until the close of the war.

In 1870 Parsons is listed in the census as a grocer at Keyser; in 1875 he was involved in real estate and timber. In the 1880 census he is listed as a speculator. He passed away at Keyser December 13, 1925, and is buried at nearby Queen's Point Cemetery.

Opposite page: These three views of New Creek (Keyser), Mineral County, were probably all taken at the same time as the bottom view by George W. Parsons in May 1865.

#1 Probably taken from Fort Fuller (later changed to Fort Kelley) which is where Potomac State College is now located. The view is facing east toward Queen's Point, Maryland, close to the small town of McCoole. Hidden at the base of the hill is the North Branch of the Potomac River. The prominent house in the center belonged to Edward Armstrong, which is the former location of the Keyser High School, now a business establishment.

#2 View looking east but much closer to Queen's Point than image #1. As it is still in West Virginia, the North Branch would be beyond the tent encampment.

#3 View taken 180 degrees from #1 and #2, again showing the Armstrong house.

NEW YORK STATE LIBRARY, THE GEN. WILLIAM W. AVERELL PAPERS VIA ANN ARONSON PHOTOGRAPHY

New Creek (Keyser), Mineral County. Camp of the 22nd Pennsylvania (Ringgold) Cavalry taken by George W. Parsons in May 1865. The first row of tents in the foreground (actually the back of the camp), from the left of the photo belonged to Company M; the second row belonged to companies L and K; the third row belonged to companies I and H; the fourth row belonged to companies G and F; and the last row belonged to companies E and D. The officer's quarters were on the far side of the long street (Mozelle Street). The large square brick mansion house with the cupola in the center of the photo was the home of Edward M. Armstrong, whose store was in the building facing the railroad at one of the crossings of the railroad at what is now Main Street. MINERAL COUNTY HISTORICAL SOCIETY

This is thought to be the earliest known photograph taken in the Charleston area. Several historians have placed this in 1863 or 1864. The men are lined up along Front Street (now Kanawha Boulevard) outfitted in some type of fraternal regalia. A few Union soldiers can be picked out in the crowd. It is not known what the occasion was. The three-story building is the Bank of the West at the corner of Front and Summers streets. E.T. Moore, who moved to Charleston from Gallipolis, Ohio sometime during the Civil War, has his printing sign displayed and apparently is painting a large sign with his name on it (the E has already been done). By June 1864, Moore was joined by his brother S. Spencer Moore. The business was known as Moore & Brother, Publishers. The S. Spencer Moore Company was in business for over 100 years. The building on the extreme right is the Laidley Drug Store with a statue of the Goddess of Health, Hygeia, and the word OIL on the column. In 1934 historian Roy Bird Cook, a man familiar with many of the veterans, said this photo was taken in the spring of 1864 at the corner of Front and Summers streets.

DAVE MOORE COLLECTION

Regimental Band of the 23rd Ohio Volunteer Infantry believed to have been taken in October 1863 in Charleston, Kanawha County. The men are standing in front of the Bank of Virginia, which stood at the corner of present-day Virginia and Summers streets. The bank was burned during the retreat of Union troops under Gen. Joseph A.J. Lightburn in September 1862. The musicians are, left to right, front row: William Arthur, Edwin Arthur, John Cramer, George Smith, Theodore Belding, Alfred Arthur, William Brown, Jim Huffman; top row: Thad Coffin, Jim String, John Oswald, Ed Spring, Eugene Coffin, Chris Miller, Arnold Issler. John Oswald was also a sketch artist and photographer.

RUTHERFORD B. HAYES LIBRARY

Field and Staff officers of the 7th West Virginia Cavalry (originally the 8th West Virginia Infantry). The men are believed to be, back row, left to right: Maj. William Gramm, Dr. James H. Rouse, Dr. Lucius L. Comstock, Capt. Jacob M. Rife, Lt. Daniel William Polsley; second row, left to right: Chaplin Andrew W. Gregg, Lt. Col. John J. Polsley, Col. John H. Oley, Maj. Hedgeman Slack, Lt. John W. Winfield; front row, left to right: Maj. Edgar B. Blundon, Thomas H. Burton, Dr. Louis V. Stanford, Lt. John McComb. Date, location and photographer unknown although it is likely the image was taken at the Partridge Gallery in Wheeling, Ohio County in 1865.

WEST VIRGINIA STATE ARCHIVES, BOYD STUTLER COLLECTION

Opposite top: The 8th West Virginia Infantry (later the 7th West Virginia Cavalry) at Buffalo, Putnam County in 1862. Members of the regimental band can be seen at the far left. Progress Mills, on the right, once stood on Front Street in Buffalo. Soldiers were quartered in the building which had standing water in the basement. Three of the soldiers died of typhoid fever, carried by mosquitoes that bred in the basement. This image was reproduced in the early 1900s as a color-tinted postcard. The original photo was a daguerrotype believed to have been taken by Dr. Claudius Mathieu Pitrat of Buffalo.

PICTORIAL HISTORIES COLLECTION

Opposite bottom: Company G, 7th West Virginia Cavalry (originally the 8th West Virginia Infantry and later mounted infantry). The three officers are Capt. James S. Cassady, First Lt. James D. Fellers and Second Lt. John E. Swaar. Most of the company was recruited in Fayette and Kanawha counties. Date, location and photographer unknown.

WEST VIRGINIA STATE ARCHIVES, BOYD STUTLER COLLECTION

This series of three rare photographs of Romney, Hampshire County, are believed to have been taken during the Civil War. The first shows the west end of town taken with the camera facing northwest. The second view is facing north, looking up High Street. It is speculated that the horses belonged to troops occupying the town. The third view is facing northeast. The large building in the center was the Potomac Seminary which is now part of the West Virginia School For The Blind. Romney exchanged hands at least 56 times during the war. Perhaps many more which are simply not recorded. Most of these involved either one side or the other simply marching into town but sometimes a skirmish would precede the occupation. "Stonewall" Jackson had his headquarters here briefly in January 1862. He threatened to resign from the Confederate army when the Secretary of War frustrated his plans for holding the town.

HAMPSHIRE COUNTY HISTORICAL SOCIETY/ROMNEY BICENTINIAL COLLECTION

N.C.O.s of Company E, 22nd New York State Militia, encamped on Camp Hill, looking toward Bolivar, October 1862.
HARPERS FERRY NATIONAL HISTORICAL PARK HF-11

Tents on west Camp Hill, facing Bolivar and Bolivar Heights, at Harpers Ferry, 1862.
HARPERS FERRY NATIONAL HISTORICAL PARK HF-493

Lower town of Harpers Ferry immediately after evacuation by the Confederates in June 1861. The 1836 railroad bridge across the Potomac River had been destroyed. The U.S. Arsenal to the right was still intact at this time.
HARPERS FERRY NATIONAL HISTORICAL PARK HF-46

Harpers Ferry from the Maryland shore, 1862, looking at lower town and Camp Hill, showing the wooden falsework on the bridge span (preliminary step in the construction of a Bollman span). Ruins of the U.S. Arsenal are to the right.
HARPERS FERRY NATIONAL HISTORICAL PARK HF-11

Union soldiers on Camp Hill at Harpers Ferry. PICTORIAL HISTORIES COLLECTION

Postwar views of the ruins of the U.S. Arsenal at Harpers Ferry, destroyed in September 1862, showing the Bollman-type bridge over the Potomac River. The cupola of John Brown's fort (the Arsenal's engine house) is visible in the lower right-hand corner of the photo below. Maryland Heights is across the river to the left.

TOP: U.S. ARMY MILITARY HISTORY INSTITUTE. BOTTOM: HARPERS FERRY HISTORICAL PARK HF-45

Soldier Art

A number of Civil War soldiers were artists, either by hobby or by trade. The results of their efforts, therefore, range from the crude and primitive of James Noble of the 1st West Virginia Cavalry to the more perfected work of John W. Oswald of the 23rd Ohio Volunteer Infantry. The detailed pictures of J. Nep Roesler of the 47th Ohio Volunteer Infantry, are among the best representations of soldier art. These men and others captured many wartime views throughout West Virginia. This may be the first time all of Roesler's lithographs have been presented in one book.

The common soldier often had time on his hands to sculpt, carve, or whittle lead bullets into representations of everything from chess pieces to gun parts or phallic symbols; to sketch crude maps of camps and battles; or to draw scenes. Some of the soldiers were such skilled artists they were able to contribute their works for publication in the national newspapers, and the works of those artists are presented in the chapter in this book on "Magazine and Newspaper Sketch Artists."

Corporal John Nepomuck Roesler

Undoubtedly, some of the best-known images of the war in West Virginia were drawn by Corp. J. Nep. Roesler, Company G (Color Guard), 47th Ohio Volunteer Infantry. His series of possibly 22 lithographs, etched on stone (only 20 have been located), of the regiment's activities in the vicinity of Gauley Bridge, Carnifex Ferry, Hawks Nest and Fayetteville rank among the best, and most recognizable, scenes of the 1861-62 campaign.

John Nep. Roesler (also spelled Rosler, Rossler and Roessler) was born circa 1826 in Baden, German. At the time of the Civil War, he was a resident of Cincinnati, Ohio, and enlisted there June 15, 1861, in Co. H, 47th Ohio Volunteer Infantry. His occupation at the time of his enlistment was "artist." He first served as a corporal in Company H and then as a corporal in Company G. He was discharged for disability February 8, 1862, at Gauley Mount, (West) Virginia and given a surgeon's certificate of disability at Cincinnati, Ohio, September 29, 1862, for loss of the left eye. He returned home and in 1862 sketched lithographs of his military experience in West Virginia. Originally sketching on stone, Roesler later mass-produced his images and sold them to returning veterans. After the war he supposedly traveled the mountains of West Virginia selling the prints. The original stones were reportedly used in his home garden in Cincinnati

The 1860 Cincinnati census includes a Frederick Roesler, born circa 1825 in Switzerland, listed as a lithographer, but no J. Nep. Roesler. On the other hand, the 1861 Cincinnati City Directory lists a J. Roessler, a lithographer at Room 2, s.w.c. of 4th and Walnut, while the 1862 Directory lists a John N. Roesler, a lithographer at 26 Jackson.

Entered according to act of Congress in the year 1865 by J. Nep. Roesler in the Clerks office of the District Court of the Southern District of Ohio

...ribed fr. nature & drawn on stone by J. Nep. Roesler Corp.l of Color Guard Comp. G. 47.th Reg.t OVUSA

Printed by Ehrgott, Forbriger & C.o, Cincin.

ADVANCE
in the Woods.

The following 20 sketches are by J. Nep Roesler.

HAWK'S NEST.

Sketched fr. nature & drawn on stone by J.Nep.Roesler Corp¹ of Color 47ᵗʰ Reg¹ ⁰V

Printed by Ehrgott, Forbriger & C⁰. Cincinnati

PICKET,
on New River Camp Anderson, W.V.

Sketched fr. nature & drawn on stone by J. Nep. Roesler Corp! of Color 47th Reg! O.V.

Printed by Ehrgott, Forbriger & C?, Cincinnati

FALL,
on the Road between Tompkin's Farm & Gauley Bridge W V

Entered according to act of Congress in the year 1862 by J. Nep. Roesler in the Clerks office of the District Court of the Southern District of Ohio

MARCH

BATTLE AT CARNIFAX FERRY

CROSSING TO FAYETTEVILLE.

LOG HOUSE ON MULLER'S FERRY

CROSSING LITTLE BIRCH RIVER

Sketched fr. nature & drawn on stone by J Nep Roesler Corp! of Color Guard Comp. G 47ᵗʰ Reg! OVUSA.   Printed by Ehrgott, Forbriger & Cᵒ. Cincinnati

VIEW FROM HAWK'S NEST

towards the East

Sketched fr. nature & drawn on stone by J. Nep Roesler Corp'l of Color Guard Comp. G 47th Reg't O.V.USA   Printed by Ehrgott, Forbriger & C°. Cincinnati

Entered according to act of Congress in the year 1861 by J. Nep. Roesler in the Clerks office of the District Court of the Southern District of Ohio

CAMP, GAULEY BRIDGE.

VIEW

Sketched fr nature & drawn on stone by I Nep Roesler Corp'l of Color Guard Comp. G 47ᵗʰ Reg'ᵗ OV. U.S.A.   Printed by Ehrgott, Forbriger & Cᵒ, Cincinnati.

PICKET ON LOVER'S LEAP
(Road to the Log House) Camp Anderson

Sketched fr nature & drawn on stone by I Nep Roesler Corp'l of Color Guard Comp. G 47ᵗʰ Reg'ᵗ OV. U.S.A.   Printed by Ehrgott, Forbriger & Cᵒ, Cincinnati.

THUNDER~STORM.
(Big Sewell Mountain)
(Reconnoissance)

Entered according to act of Congress in the year 1862 by J Nep. Roesller in the Clerks office of the District Court for the Southern District of Ohio

Sketched ft. nature & drawn on stone by J Nep Roesller Corpl of Color Guard Comp. G 47ᵗʰ Reg't OV USA   Printed by Ehrgott, Forbriger & Cᵒ. Cincinnati.

VIEW FROM HAWK'S NEST
towards the West

Entered according to act of Congress in the year 1862 by J Nep. Roesller in the Clerks office of the District Court of the Southern District of Ohio

Sketched ft. nature & drawn on stone by J Nep Roesller Corpl of Color Guard Comp. G 47ᵗʰ Reg't OV USA   Printed by Ehrgott, Forbriger & Cᵒ. Cincinnati

SKIRMISHING,
New River

Entered according to act of Congress in the year 1861 by J. Nep. Roesler in the Clerks office of the District Court of the Southern District of Ohio

Sketched in details & drawn on stone by J. Nep. Roesler Corp'l of Color Guard Comp. G 47th Reg't OVI U.S.A

Printed by Ehrgott, Forbriger & C°, Cincinnati.

PICKETS IN THE WOODS

after the Engagement, near the Drill Ground, C Andrsn

Entered according to act of Congress in the year 1861 by J. Nep. Roesler in the Clerks office of the District Court of the Southern District of Ohio

Sketched in nature & drawn on stone by J. Nep. Roesler Corp'l of Color Guard Comp. G 47th Reg't OVI U.S.A

Printed by Ehrgott, Forbriger & C°, Cincinnati.

PICKETS ON THE ROAD

fr Cp Andrsn to Tompkins' Farm

Sketched fr nature & drawn on stone by J. Nep. Roesler Corp'l of Color 47th Reg' OV

Printed by Ehrgott, Forbriger & C°, Cincinnati

TOMPKIN'S FARM.
(Camp Gauley Mount.)

Entered according to act of Congress in the year 1862 by J. Nep. Roesler in the Clerks office of the District Court of the Southern District of Ohio

Sketched fr nature & drawn on stone by J. Nep. Roesler Corp'l of Color Guard Camp Gauley 47th Reg' OV M'tia

Printed by Ehrgott, Forbriger & C°, Cincinnati

Entered according to act of Congress in the year 1862 by J. Nep. Roesler in the Clerks office of the District Court of the Southern District of Ohio

FALL NEAR THE LOG HOUSE.
Camp Anderson.

Crude sketch of the rebel fortifications at Rich Mountain, Randolph County. This is attributed to Pvt. James I. O'Hara, Company B, 3rd Ohio Volunteer Infantry.

General Floyd's Army of the Kanawha recrossing the Gauley River following the Battle of Carnifex Ferry. This was sketched by Confederate artist W.D. Washington who was with the 51st Virginia Infantry. (See Washington's biography in the color section.) PICTORIAL HISTORIES COLLECTION

John B. Floyd's Confederate artillery preparing to shell the camp of Gen. William S. Rosecrans at Gauley Bridge in November 1861. It was sketched by W.D. Washington and re-sketched by William Ludwell Sheppard for The Century *magazine.*

THE CENTURY MAGAZINE (BATTLES AND LEADERS)

Fayetteville, Fayette County, drawn to represent September 10, 1862. The town was attacked by Confederate forces under the command of Gen. William W. Loring later that day. This drawing and the next four were possibly done by a member of the 34th Ohio Volunteer Infantry or the 2nd West Virginia Cavalry. The style is similar to that of John F.E. Hillen of the 34th O.V.I.

TIM McKINNEY COLLECTION

The Battle of Charleston, Kanawha County, Sept. 13, 1862. 34th, 37th, 44th and 47th Ohio Volunteer Infantry regiments cutting the cables on the Elk River suspension bridge.

WEST VIRGINIA STATE ARCHIVES

"Fording the Ohio River - September 13th, 1862 - 34th, 37th, & 44th O.V.I., 4th, 9th & 13th [West] V.V.I., and 2nd [West] V.C." This image depicts the retreating Federal forces of Gen. Joseph A.J. Lightburn from the Kanawha Valley. This would be in the vicinity of present-day Ravenswood, Jackson County.
WEST VIRGINIA STATE ARCHIVES

"Kanawha - Picket- 2nd [West] Virginia Cavalry - September 29, 1862." This image depicts the return of Federal troops to the Kanawha Valley following the departure of Confederate Gen. William W. Loring.
WEST VIRGINIA STATE ARCHIVES

Barboursville, Cabell County, November 1861 BARBOURSVILLE CHAPTER D.A.R.

Opposite: Between July and August 1861 Federal forces constructed an earth and log fortification here as a means of controlling the Staunton-Parkersburg Turnpike. On September 12, 1861, Confederate troops under General R.E. Lee attempted to capture the fort. Union troops under Col. N. Kimball engaged the Confederates within one-half mile of Cheat Summit Fort. An uncoordinated battle resulted in with-drawal of the Confederate forces. An associated action against Camp Elkwater also met with little success. In the fall of 1861 the fort was used as a staging area for actions against Confederate Camps Bartow and Top of Allegheny. Cheat Summit Fort served as an encampment for Federal troops in the winter of 1861–62. Occupants of the fort suffered terribly from bitter cold and damp conditions. The position was difficult to maintain and supply. Harsh weather increased the losses of men and horses. These factors contributed to the decision to abandon the fort in April of 1862.

Drawing by a member of the 2nd West Virginia Infantry of Cheat Mountain Summit near Cheat Bridge, Randolph County. Its elevation was the highest of any encampment occupied by Union troops during the war. PICTORIAL HISTORIES COLLECTION

A primitive drawing of the Union fortifications on Cheat Mountain Summit.
RANDOLPH COUNTY HISTORICAL SOCIETY

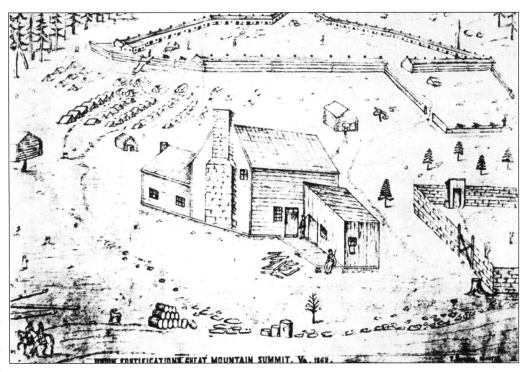

River bridge at Coalsmouth (St. Albans), Kanawha County, drawn from memory by John W. Overshiner, Company G., 11th West Virginia Infantry. The bridge was built in 1832 over the Coal River as part of the James River and Kanawha Turnpike. It was destroyed in July 1861 by retreating Confederate troops. It was rebuilt ten years later, and the current Main Street bridge was built on the same location. Overshiner was born circa 1818 and in 1860 was a carriage and wagon maker at Coalsmouth. He enlisted in the Federal army on May 23, 1862 and was discharged, probably for age or health at an unknown date. He appears in the 1870 Kanawha County census but is not in the 1880 census, indicating that he probably died sometime in that decade.

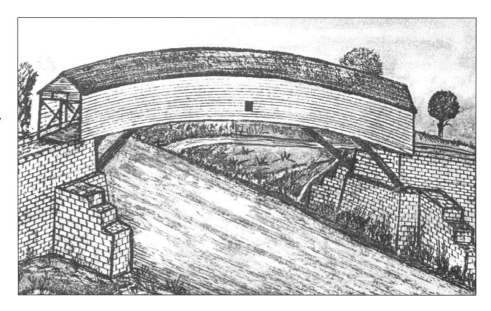

BILL WINTZ COLLECTION

Sketches made by Sgt. Maj. Lucian Gray, 1st (West) Virginia Volunteer Infantry, while his unit was occupying Camp Mechanicsburg Gap on Mill Ridge. The camp, located three miles west of Romney on U.S. Route 50 is being developed in 2000 by the Division of Natural Resources as a state park.

HAMPSHIRE COUNTY HISTORICAL SOCIETY

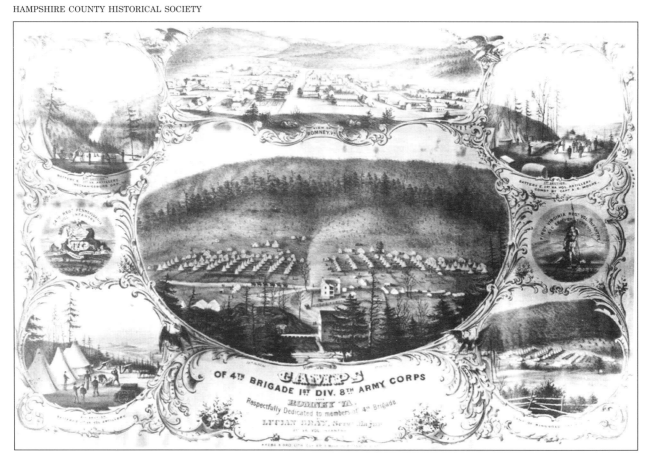

Silver plate presented to Mrs. R. B. Hayes on Hayes' silver wedding anniversary Dec. 30, 1877, by the members of the 23rd O.V.I. at Washington, D.C. The log cabin is the one pictured in the drawing below.

RUTHERFORD B. HAYES LIBRARY

Possibly a war period drawing of the log cabin of Col. Rutherford B. Hayes at Camp Reynolds, Kanawha Falls, Fayette County. This was the winter headquarters of his 23rd Ohio Volunteer Infantry. The name of the artist is in the lower left corner and appears to be either F. Mitterand or F. Milfurand. There is no soldier by this name in the index of either Ohio or Union West Virginia soldiers, indicating this could possibly be a postwar sketch.

RUTHERFORD B. HAYES LIBRARY

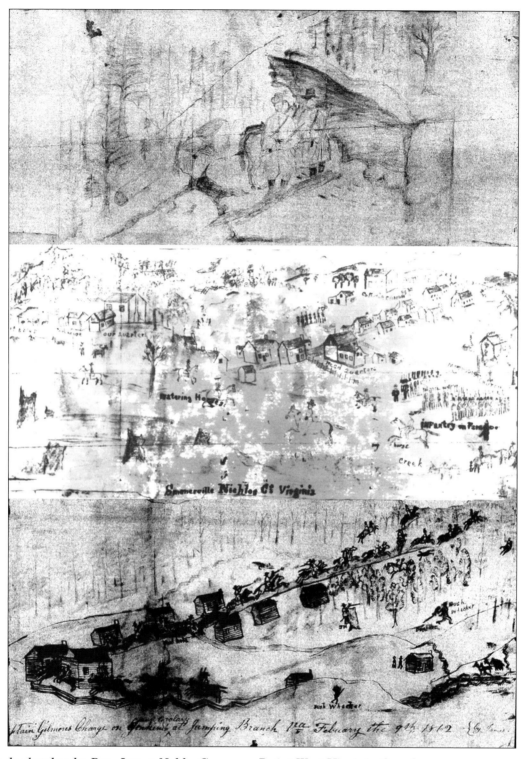

Three crude sketches by Pvt. James Noble, Company B, 1st West Virginia Cavalry:

(Top) Capt. Gilmore's Cavalry on picket near Bwices(Bowyer's ?) Ferry near the New River.

(Middle) Summersville, Nicholas County. In 1956 historian W.G. Brown said this sketch was made from a point on the hill east of the school. The branch where horses are watering is Arbuckle Branch about where it crosses Route 39.

(Bottom) Capt. Gilmore's charge on [Albert G.] Jenkins' Cavalry at Jumping Branch, Summers County, [West] Va., February 9, 1862.

These sketches were probably made during the winter of 1861–62.

CARNIFEX FERRY STATE PARK COLLECTION

The Two James Nobles

James Noble was born circa 1828 in Ireland, the son of James and Rosa Noble. In his early years he crossed the Atlantic to Canada, then to West Alexander, Washington County, Pennsylvania, where he engaged for some time in the manufacture of footwear. On Feb. 6,1855 he married Sarah J. Lavey. At the outbreak of the war he enlisted as a private in Company B, 1st West Virginia Cavalry, and for a time served as an orderly on the staff of Gen. William S. Rosecrans. In January 1862 he wrote a letter from Beckley, Raleigh County, requesting a transfer for himself and 11 other members of the regiment as he felt their abilities were being wasted. Noble was killed on March 14, 1862, by bushwackers while on a scouting expedition in West Virginia. Noble was a favorite with his comrades and the G.A.R. post in West Alexander was named in his honor.

James C. Noble was born circa 1842 also in Washington County, Pennsylvania. He enlisted in Company B, 1st West Virginia Cavalry as well and served as a saddler. He was captured at Port Republic, Virginia on Sept. 27, 1862, and died at the Andersonville prison camp in March or April 1865. It is assumed that the artist in question was the former James Noble mentioned.

Charles Reidel

Charles Reidel was born May 25, 1837, in Friedberg, Silesia, Austria. He immigrated to the United States, and when the Civil War broke out he enlisted at Columbus, Ohio, as a private in Company H, 12th Ohio Volunteer Infantry, on April 24, 1861, for three months service. His occupation was listed as a machinist, and on June 19, 1861, he reenlisted in the regiment for three years service. From November 1862 to February 1863 he was on detached duty as a bugler for Capt. Seth Simmond's Independent Kentucky Battery, and on May 1, 1863 he was appointed Principal Musician for Company H, 12th Ohio and transferred to Field and Staff. Reidel was mustered out with the 12th Ohio on July 11, 1864. He married Mary Fritz at Ripley, Brown County, Ohio, October or November 1864. After the war he resided in Ohio and in 1890 at Minerva, Kentucky. He filed for a pension claiming that in the summer of 1887 he contracted a disease of the rectum, probably caused by irregularity of the bowels. Reidel died on March 29, 1911, at Woodlawn, Nelson County, Kentucky.

Camp of the 12th Ohio Volunteer Infantry at Fayetteville, Fayette County in April 1863 showing: (A) Fort Scammon, (B) Battery McMullen (C) Camp of the 12th O.V.I. (D) Fayetteville Courthouse. The artist was Charles Riedel, Company H, 12th O.V.I.

WEST VIRGINIA STATE ARCHIVES

Camp of the 12 th Regt O.V.I. at Fayetteville Va April 1863.
A. Fort Scammon. — B. Battery McMullan.— C. Camp of the 12 Regt O.VI.—D. Fayetteville Courthouse.

"The Last Attack on Fayetteville, W.Va." in Fayette County. Although the picture credits this event as having transpired on May 21, 1863 it actually took place on May 19. The artist is unknown and some sources have speculated that this image was drawn in the postwar period. Although there is a legend with a lettering system, most of the letters are not visible. Purportedly the legend reads: (A) Attacking Confederate Force McCausland's 36th, 6 companies 60th Virginia, and Bryan's Battery, 4 pieces; (B) Defending Federal Fort Toland White's 12th Ohio and 2 pieces McMullin's Battery; (C) 12th Ohio, 2 companies, and 2 pieces McMullin's Battery, Fort Sieber; (D) Colonel White's headquarters, 12th Ohio; (E) County jail; (F) Court House; (G) Camp 12th Ohio; (H) 13th West Virginia Regiment; (J) Fort Scammon; (K) Federal fort; (L) Federal fort; (M) Raleigh road; (N) Gauley Bridge Road.

WEST VIRGINIA STATE ARCHIVES

CAMP OF 5TH VIRGINIA VOL. INFANTRY, U. S. A.

FALLS OF KANAWHA, WEST VIRGINIA.   1864.

OUR CHAPLAIN

Gives each of us a copy of this Engraving, to show our friends the way we sing and hold meetings in camp. He desires us to tell them to pray for us and him, that we may prove faithful to our country and our God, and not be found wanting in any day of temptation and trial.

Camp of the 5th [West] Virginia Volunteer Infantry, U.S.A. at Kanawha Falls, Fayette County, in 1864. The sketch shows Chaplain Joseph Little playing a portable field organ for the soldiers. The sketch is undoubtedly based upon the accompanying photo of Chaplain Little. Backmark on the photo is J.Q.A. Tresize, Zanesville. Note the rifle behind the chaplain. This view is different from the one in the reprint of Loyal West Virginians.

SKETCH: WEST VIRGINIA STATE ARCHIVES

PHOTO: L.M. STRAYER COLLECTION

THE KNAPSACK.

ORGAN OF THE FIFTH VA VOL INFANTRY, U.S.A.

Vol. I. ...ridge, West Va, Thursday, Oct. 8, 186... No. 6.

For the ...
"GAY AND HAPPY."

Girls whom are gay and happy
Knowing we have a woman's ...
We'll but well a-boing-sick down...
But wait and le...

Gay and happy; hear the army...
None but fools get married now...
Valliant men have all enlisted,
And to cowards we'll not bow...

We're the girls so gay and happy,
Waiting for the end of strife...
Better share a soldier's ration,
Than to be a coward's ...

For the gay and for the ...
We're as constant ...
But the man that ...
Never can o'think ...

PRAIRIE MILLS, IOWA

HISTORY
OF THE
Fifth Regiment Va. Vol....

[CONTINUED FROM NO. 5.]

Reader, citizen reader, I mean...

actly how the rebel army can be captured,
and a e sup ised at the igno ance of the
Fede al Gene als fo not seeing throug it
at once. You have seen young men
with a few st agg ing, sickly hai s on their
uppe lip, (they call it moustache) with a
snow-white si t bosom, (the wa... d
d aws desti ute rations f om ...
a ment,) with a head that Nap...
nere mistake fo his ma shal s ...
hea d these p oo , pitiable, con...
tailgs explain how they would the...
have captu ed Lee and his ar...
Vicksbu g might have been ta...
befo e it was; and who e in Gene...
crans made a g eat failu e at Ch...
ga. The opinions of all such me...
neath the contempt of the so...
ought to be snee ed at by the se...
ized. Soldie s say but little ...
qualifi ations of the Gene als; ...
ask is to know thei o de s. Cit...
pecially those who have not the coun...
fight, have no right to an opinion ...
ing an offi e — not that any officer ...
not be held to a st ct accounta...
all the acts, and that he should ...
criti ised for his failu es; but tha...
cism should be made by his supe io...
not by men who a e as igno ant of his...
ti e s duties as any dumb anim l ...
field. Any numbe of Majo Gene ...
be found in the civic ranks who...
ing to thei opinions, could have ...
rebellion f om existence in a ...
had an oppo tunity been given th...
lli ... ately fo the gove nment, ...
... self of the se ices of the...

had taken anothe position a few miles
fu the on.

F om St asbu g to Ha isonbu g the incidents of one day we e but the epetition
of the p e ceding except a te ible hail
sto m at Woodstock, a epetition of which
was, by no means, desi able.

"A STEAK OF CHIVALRY."—One of the most
inhuman acts that has been pe petrated
since the war commenced, was attempted
to be carried out by the ebels on the
night of the eva uation of Fo t Wagne .
Acco ding to the statement of a wounded
man, disco ve ed in the bomb p oof, he had
been lying in a dying condition fo fou
days. The ebels efused to give him even
a swallow of wate to quen h his thi st,
and told him when they left that he could
not possibly live and had bette befo e
dying, do as much fo the cause as lay in
his power. That he might benefit by this
advi e, they placed in his hand a string attached to a fuze communi ating with the
magazine befo e alluded to, with inst uc-
tions to pull it when the fo t was well fill-
d with Yankees, and so send them all
... But the
wounded rebel, although almost dead when
ou men entered the fo t, had a faint hope
that pe haps he might live if p ope ly attended, and gave that as a reason fo not
pulling the st ing. He was taken to an ambulance, and died while being conveyed
to the hospital.

The othe day, a f iend wishing to
teach my little th ee-year old Susie the
hymn beginning: "I want to be an angel,"
told her to repeat the fi st line, when she
looked up, and with animation exclaimed:

INCIDENTS.

... the crossing could be effected it would be of
good deal of importance, and if Col. Zeig
felt sure he could make it, he might go ahead
The Colonel gave the order and his men sip go
ahead. It was a dangerous crossing, but by 4
o'clock that day the regiment and train were
all over, with the loss only of one wagon and
part of the harness. The wagon-master, Jo.
Shepard, came near being drowned in his efforts
to save the wagon, but after swimming under
water between the horse' legs and through the
wagon wheel, he came out right side up. We
were followed rapidly by the balance of the
brigade, and the next day were all on the march
towa d Franklin.

DuBeck's battery was in our brigade. Du-
Beck had a fine lot of high-spirited horses.
When the first gun was in the middle of the
river, the rough bottom and swift torrent rendered the horses unmanageable, they were drawn
ed and the others cut loose and taken out, and
the splendid 12 pdr. was left in the river. None
of the officers could tell what should be done
... until the water ... The 5th Va. would...
ssacked on the other side; they saw the em-
barrassment of the officers, and a number of
Co. B. boys with a shout rushed into the stream,
hanging by a rope to support themselves in the
swift current, attached the rope to the gun and
in five minutes had it safely on dry land. This
decided the work of the day. The General
concluded to get all over at once, and the ...
am was in motion twenty-four hours sooner
than it would have been but fo the prompt and
energetic work of the Fifth Va. And in this...
... the young effo ts of ...

THE KNAPSACK,
ORGAN OF THE 5th VA VOL. INFANTRY

L. G. DOWNTAIN, - - - - Editor

is published every Thursday morning by the 5th Va Publishing Association.

Price 15 cents a month and 5 cents per single copy, payable in advance to the carrier.

All letters relating to business, should be addressed to the "Board of Directors."

Contributions must be sent to the editor and addressed as follows: "Editor Knapsack, Gauley Bridge, West Va."

BOARD OF DIRECTORS.

Capt. W. T. McQuigg, *President.*
Capt. J. P. Watmer, *Secretary.*
Lt.-Col. W. H. Enochs,
Lieut. Samuel Jones,
Q. M. Sergt. C. B. Webb.

DIRECTORY
OF THE
5th Regiment Va. Vol. Infantry.

FIELD AND STAFF.

Colonel	- - - -	A. A. Tomlinson,
Lt.-Colonel	- - -	W. H. Enochs,
Major	- - -	Vacant,
Surgeon	- - - -	P. Randall,
Sen. Assist. Surgeon	-	D. Mayer,
Jr. Assist. Surgeon	-	C. D. Dally,
Adjutant	- - -	P. Davey,
Quartermaster	- -	D. Ramsdell,
Chaplain	- - - -	J. Little,

NON-COMMISSIONED STAFF.

Serg't. Maj.	- - - -	P. L. Hersey,
Q. M. Sergeant	- -	C. B. Webb,
Commissary Sergeant	-	James Darling,
Hospital Steward	- -	A. B. Carnahan,

LINE OFFICERS.

COMPANY "A."

Captain	- - -	Mark Poore,
1st Lieutenant	- -	Wm. Shelling,
2nd	- -	D. J. Thomas.

COMPANY "B."

Captain	- -	R. B. McCall,
1st Lieutenant	- -	J. F. Bancroft,
2nd	- -	Vacant.

COMPANY "C."

Captain	- -	W. T. McQuigg,
1st Lieutenant	- -	Guy Rowe,
2nd	- -	Wm. Rowe.

COMPANY "D."

Captain	- -	J. B. Baxell,
1st Lieutenant	- -	H. C. Neff,
2nd	- -	A. W. Miller.

COMPANY "E."

Captain	- -	H. Willis,
1st Lieutenant	- -	H. H. Wolcott,
2nd	- -	Wm. Willis.

COMPANY "F."

Captain	- -	E. E. Merriman,
Lieutenant	- -	W. H. H. Ess,
	- -	A. Pace.

COMPANY "G."

Captain	- -	J. P. Watmer,
Lieutenant	- -	B. Johnston,
	- -	Vacant.

COMPANY "H."

Captain	- -	H. Kuocha,
Lieutenant	- -	S. McClung,

For the Knapsack.

REMEMBER THEM.

If ever anybody was and is entitled to the gratitude of a nation, it is the American soldier, who went forth to fight for his country's cause, and under his country's flag. The small pittance of $13 which he gets a month as his pay, is but like a drop in the ocean for his services in camp, on the march and on the battlefield. The memorando of the correspondent and the pen of the historian is not able to describe the inconveniences and hardships, the privations and endurance he has to undergo while in the service. But look into the hospitals and upon the sick beds of soldiers at home, and there you will find ruined constitutions and suffering beings, the riches of tedious campaigns and bloody battles. Look, if you can, into the graves that have sprung up in fearful numbers down at the enemy's South and at home in the far North—they contain many a dear one of whom parents were once proud; many a one whose grave will never be moistened by the tears of his widow and orphans; many a one who was the pride of society and the church—You cannot call them back, but you can compensate the living soldier somewhat for his services, relieve the sufferings of the sick and honor the glorious dead by remembering their relatives, their friends and families, many of whom perhaps are now suffering. You, ye at home, remember them, and you will do a work, for which God and man alike ...

Winter is at the door and with it its expensive living. $13 a month is too small a sum for many a soldier's family to live on; they must therefore suffer if you at home do not help them along. Knowing his family provided for, the soldier can and will do ... of the duty which our country is in need ... faithfully and gladly, and thus the good ... our Union and Liberty and the putting down of the infamous rebellion can go on ... assurance of glorious results—results which will ... all of us at the proper time.

The thousands of brave ... who are now nearly spread all over the ... of the States, look upon you at home to provide, as much as is in your power, for their needy families and in doing that you pay the tribute of gratitude to the living as well as the dead of the Stars and Stripes noble defenders.

W. S.

For the Knapsack.

PROFANITY.

... the habit of swearing. To what a very great extent is this practiced, regardless of morality, decency, law, or any thing pertaining thereto. It would be well for those persons addicted to this ungentlemanly habit, to consider one moment this fact, that at some future time they will again return to civil life, and be seeking the society of ladies; then they will find it difficult indeed to abstain from the vulgar habit of swearing, and we presume no gentleman would like a reprimand or be sneered at on account of giving way to a habit. It is a fact evident to the thinking mind of every rational man, that habits can be cultivated until they become almost nature itself. A man may cultivate a habit or passion until it will over rule his better judgment. A person may become so accustomed to swearing ... be unconscious of what he is saying; then he is sure to insult the ladies, for nothing is so unbecoming a gentleman as to use profane language in their presence. It has been said by some writers that immodest language is generally used by the low and uneducated. This is true in a general sense, but not in every particular ... very often hear the men of letters make use of profane and obscene language when ... expected but should be an example ... of refinement. Dr. Franklin says:—

"Immodest words admit of no defence."

That want of decency is want of sense." Well, we think a person ... decent and yet very sensible of those ... it would be impossible to be deemed ... any use at all. Well, in that case ... have to be governed by the old ... given, little required."

Now we hope our brave ... boys will consider the impropriety of ... swearing, and for the future, so far as ... refrain from this unbecoming practice ...

H. C. N.

---

and O. ye Democrats, there is one over in Canada exiled for not voting one man nor dollar to carry on this abolition war inaugurated by the President, and expressing his sentiment in favor of armed traitors of the South now in rebellion against the United States. Now my friends, I tell you that he will be elected governor of the state of Ohio, and he will establish a new dispensation for you.

Pugh went on in his usual manner, making false assertions against the Administration, and justifying the rebel states in their war, until the boys from the hospital in this place could stand it no longer, and they gave traitor Pugh the lie. They sneered, and hissed and groaned until the traitor ceased his lying and suddenly strangely disappeared. Had it not been for the military authority here, I believe Pugh would have been taken out and killed with as much deliberation as they would kill a guerrilla in the hills of West Virginia. He may thank his stars that the military was there that day holding violence in check, for when they made a demonstration of a Vallandigham flag, the boys tore it up in less time than a toad could snap a fly, and then each hurrying in hot haste to prevent bloodshed that every boy got a piece of the flag.

On the 26th of Sept. came Mr Hutchin, Hon B. F. Wade, and Col Anderson, and planted their batteries about 11 o'clock, opened a galling fire on Vallandigham, Pugh and the whole traitor crew, and for four long hours I think such a roar of cannonading never was heard at the battles of Antietam, Bull Run or Cedar Mountain. Charging their batteries extra they opened an enfilading fire on the whole line of traitors in Ohio; and when the firing ceased there was not a Vallandighammer to be found in the whole crowd of 5,000.

There is calm, quiet determination on the citizens of Gallia county, to vote traitors out of office instead of in, and those who were copperhead, before the meeting are now for Brough.

After all this strife, looking at the future of our glorious country, we see her with ...

...

HUGH WILL ...

Medical Department.

Dr. D. MAYER - - - - - - E...

SLEEP.

Death from old age has been compared to going asleep, never to awaken again in this world, in consequence the transition is easy to a kind consideration of the phenomena of sleep, nature's soft nurse, so necessary to our existence. Disease or madness must be the result of a long continued absence of this great restorer; so ... said Byron in his last illness. Sir Benjamin Brodie mentions the case of a gentleman who from intense anxiety, passed six entire days without sleep. At the end of this time he became afflicted with illusions of such a ... that it was necessary to place him in confinement. After sometime he recovered perfectly. He had never shown any signs of mental derangement before, nor had any of his family, and has never been similarly afflicted since. Those who have been subject to cruel ... have declared that the most intolerable ... deprivation of sleep; and as this was one of the modes of treating the unhappy old women who fell into the hands of the witch-finders ... by confessions they made. The sick frequently has recourse to stimulants, which ... used, remove, for a time, the uneasiness and languor occasioned by want of sleep. But ... porary relief is dearly purchased, and they ... have recourse to alcohol on such ... should know that it does not create ... power, but only enables the recipients ... that which is left, leaving them in more ... rest than ever, when the stimulus has ...

Col. Frederick Poschner

Frederick Poschner, born circa 1820, was a native of Hungary and one of the heroes of the Hungarian revolution of 1848. As an officer in the Austrian army, he was called an "Austrian by birth but American by choice," and he had a strong reputation for gallantry and efficiency acquired in the Hungarian Revolution. Physically, Poschner was of "low stature, with a well built figure and a quick inquisitive eye. He was a rapid speaker and a well meaning man."

At the outbreak of the American Civil War, while at Cincinnati, Ohio, he was made colonel of the 47th Ohio Volunteer Infantry. He was a rigid disciplinarian on military matters, which made him a bit unpopular with his men, mostly Germans. Poschner spent the winter of 1861–62 in the vicinity of "Gauley Mount" (Tompkins farm) near Gauley Bridge. In December 1861 Ellen Tompkins wrote a letter from the farm stating, "He [Poschner] is drawing me a picture of the farm as a great encampment, as it is." A portion of this drawing exists in the Tompkins Papers and, upon comparison, is obviously a version of the well known drawing of the camp by Corp. J. Nep. Roesler of the 47th Ohio, leading some to believe they may be one and the same man, but such is not true.

Poschner's health deteriorated, and on March 25, 1862, Lt. Col. Lyman S. Elliot of the regiment reported Poschner could no longer hold a pen in his hand and was "not expected to live the day." He did survive, though, and tendered his resignation July 17, 1862 due to ill health. He died August 11, 1873, at the National Asylum for D.V.S. in Dayton, Ohio.

Although the sketch above is attributed to Col. Frederick Poschner of the 47th Ohio Volunteer Infantry, it is obviously a segment of the sketch of the Tompkins farm by Corp. J. Nep Roesler of the 47th O.V. I.
VIRGINIA MAGAZINE OF HISTORY AND BIOGRAPHY

Mount Gauley
Colored sketch by Joseph Goodloe Tompkins.

John William Oswald

John William Oswald was born October 5, 1842, at Ashland, Ashland County, Ohio, the son of Levi and Caroline Oswald. On June 7, 1861, he enlisted in Company G, 23rd Ohio Volunteer Infantry as a private and later served as a musician in the regimental band. He was mustered out of service July 6, 1864, and married Cordelia Cordell at Ashland on May 3, 1865. On his military pension papers dated 1897, he mentioned he suffered from "rheumatism, neuralgia, and general disability, result of pneumonia he had in May 1895." On these various papers, written from his home at Toledo, Ohio, he repeatedly listed his occupation as photographer or artist. In 1916 his left eye was diseased and removed. The following year his wife passed away. John W. Oswald died at Toledo on September 26, 1926. He drew a number of pictures while on duty in West Virginia.

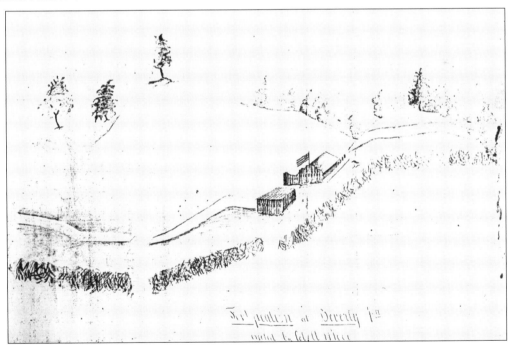

A rare sketch titled "Fortification at Beverly, [West] Virginia, erected by Col. A. Moor." It was probably made while Col. Augustus Moor of the 28th Ohio Volunteer Infantry commanded the post between July and November 1863 and is signed "Heer" [left corner], probably Capt. Arnold Heer, Co. K, 28th Ohio Volunteer Infantry. At the age of 33, Heer was wounded in the Battle of Piedmont, Virginia, June 3, 1864. AUGUSTUS MOOR PAPERS, RATTERMAN COLLECTION, UNIVERSITY OF ILLINOIS-CHAMPAIGN

Camp Reynolds, Kanawha Falls, Fayette County, the 1862–63 winters quarters of Col. Rutherford B. Hayes and his 23rd Ohio Volunteer Infantry. Sketched by John W. Oswald, Company G, 23rd O.V.I. This sketch is the basis for the painting of the same scene by Oswald on page 205.
RUTHERFORD B. HAYES LIBRARY

Map of Camp Reynolds, Kanawha Falls, Fayette County. DON MINDERMANN

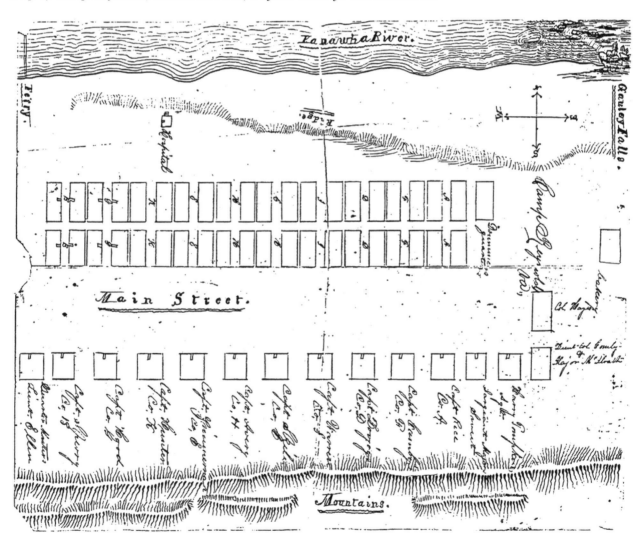

War period drawing of a mill at Kanawha Falls, Fayette County. The artist is unknown, but the style is very similiar to that of John W. Oswald. RUTHERFORD B. HAYES LIBRARY #519

"Tompkins' farm, West Va." in Fayette County near Gauley Bridge. This was the Federal encampment at "Gauley Mount," the home of Confederate Col. Christopher Q. Tompkins of the 22nd Virginia Infantry. Sketched by John W. Oswald. RUTHERFORD B. HAYES LIBRARY #3926

From a Sketch by J. W Oswald, Co. "G," 23d O. V. I.

Tompkins' Farm, West Va.

"The Battle of Cloyd's Mountain, Virginia - May 9, 1864" - near Dublin, Virginia. Although this battle did not take place on West Virginia soil, it has often been mistaken as West Virginia by many writers, possibly due to the large number of state soldiers in both armies as well as its close proximity to West Virginia. Written notes on a copy at the Virginia Historical Society at Richmond record men in line at or near the left of the picture as the "Charge of the 23rd O.V.I. - should be further to the right," and the men to the left of the road are designated as "3rd and 4th Pa. Reserves. - 600 men - repulsed." John W. Oswald's initials appear in the lower right corner. Confederate Gen. Albert G. Jenkins from Cabell County was killed in this battle. RUTHERFORD B. HAYES LIBRARY #724

1864 view of the camp of the 5th New York Heavy Artillery on Camp Hill, Harpers Ferry. The encampment lies adjacent to the commanding officer's or armory superintendent's house. Temporary military structures, barracks, troops, camp layout, laundry facility, and camp followers "laundresses" are all visible. Drawn by Ward S. Day, Company C, 5th N.Y.H.A. Lithograph published by E. Sachse & Co., 1865. HARPERS FERRY NATIONAL HISTORICAL PARK HF #20

Battlefields and Campsites drawn by Soldiers

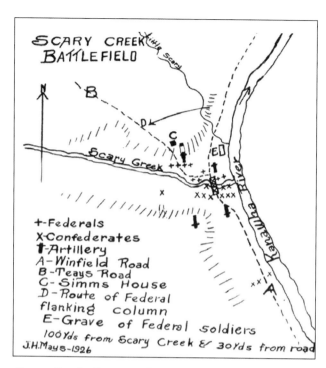

Many maps of battlefields and campsites were drawn by official military authorities and newspaper correspondents, but the most sought-after are those works sketched by the rank and file soldiers, often found in their letters and diaries. We have included some of the better examples of these as pertaining to West Virginia.

Scary Creek, Putnam County, drawn in 1926 by veteran James H. Mays, Co. F, 22nd Virginia Infantry, CSA.

Sketch, probably by Corp. Clarkson Fogg, Co. C, 4th West Virginia Infantry of "Camp Lightburn, seen from the rear - Ceredo House." This was the 1861–62 winter camp of the 4th West Virginia Infantry at Ceredo, Wayne County. Fogg was killed in action at Vicksburg, Mississippi on May 19, 1863. BRIAN KESTERSON COLLECTION

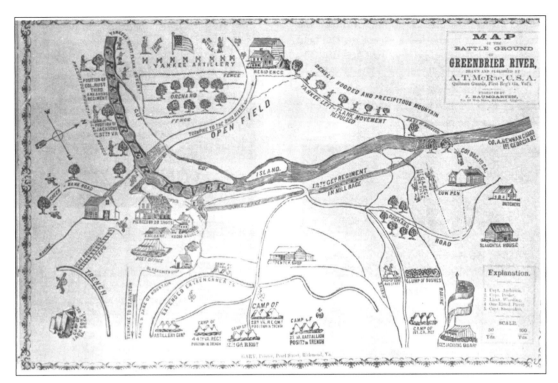

A map of the battleground along the Greenbrier River in Pocahontas County, drawn by A.T.McRae of the Quitman Guards, First Regiment, Georgia Volunteers. The turnpike shown on the left is the strategic Parkersburg-Staunton Turnpike which connected the Virginia Valley with the Ohio River. The pike to the east passed by Top of Allegheny, the highest campsite (in elevation) during the war and scene of a battle December 13, 1861, in which the entrenched Confederate forces repulsed a Union attack with a loss of 137 killed and wounded. This area was known as Camp Bartow near the present-day community of Bartow.

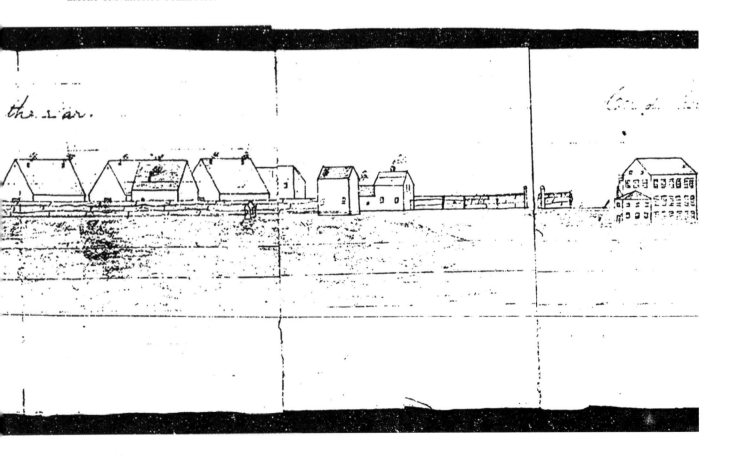

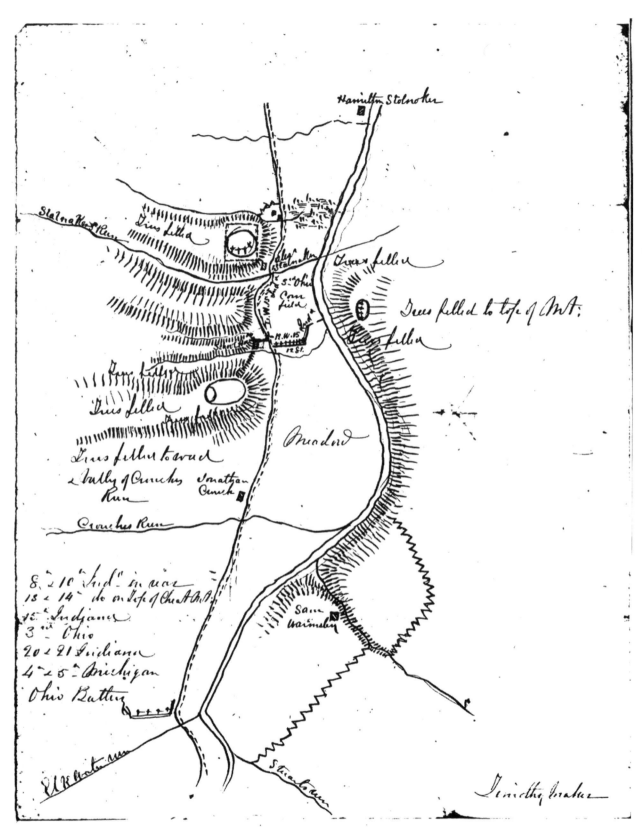

Map of the Federal camps around Elkwater, Randolph County. The name in the right-hand corner appears as Timothy Maker, perhaps a Union soldier. VIRGINIA HISTORICAL SOCIETY

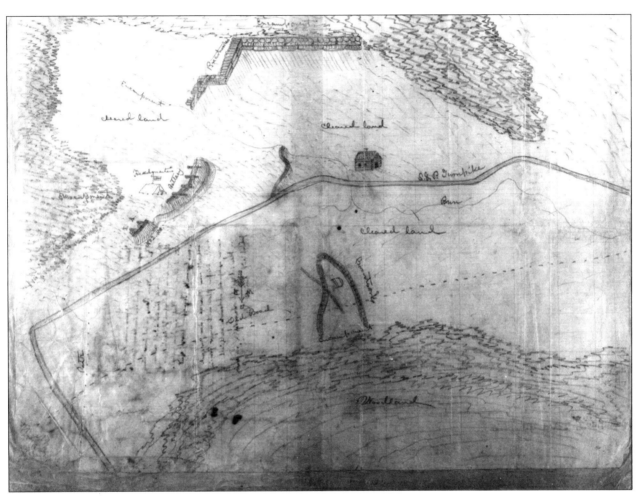

Rare, previously unpublished map of the Confederate fortifications at Laurel Hill, Barbour County. The sketch was apparently captured by the Federal troops of Gen. William S. Rosecrans. Camp Laural Hill was established by Confederate Gen. Robert S. Garnett with some 4,000–6,000 troops. A battle was fought at nearby Belington July 8, 1861. GEN. WILLIAM S. ROSECRANS COLLECTION, UNIVERSITY OF CALIFORNIA-LOS ANGELES.

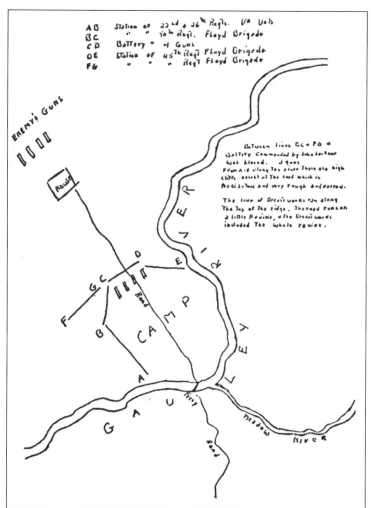

This is the only known Confederate map of the Carnifex Ferry Battlefield. It was drawn by Maj. Isaac Noyes Smith of the 22nd Virginia Infantry in his diary. He has made some possible mistakes as he has the point F–G defended by the 45th Virginia when in fact it was probably defended by portions of the 36th and 51st Virginia. He also calls Lt. Thomas E. Jackson by the name of "John" Jackson. JACOB D. COX PAPERS, MUDD LIBRARY, OBERLIN COLLEGE

This crude sketch of the Carnifex Ferry battlefield was drawn by Maj. Rutherford B. Hayes of the 23rd Ohio in his diary. The future President of the United States admitted he had a bad view and the map was out of perspective, showing Federal regiments practically to the exact rear of Confederate General John B. Floyd. RUTHERFORD B. HAYES LIBRARY

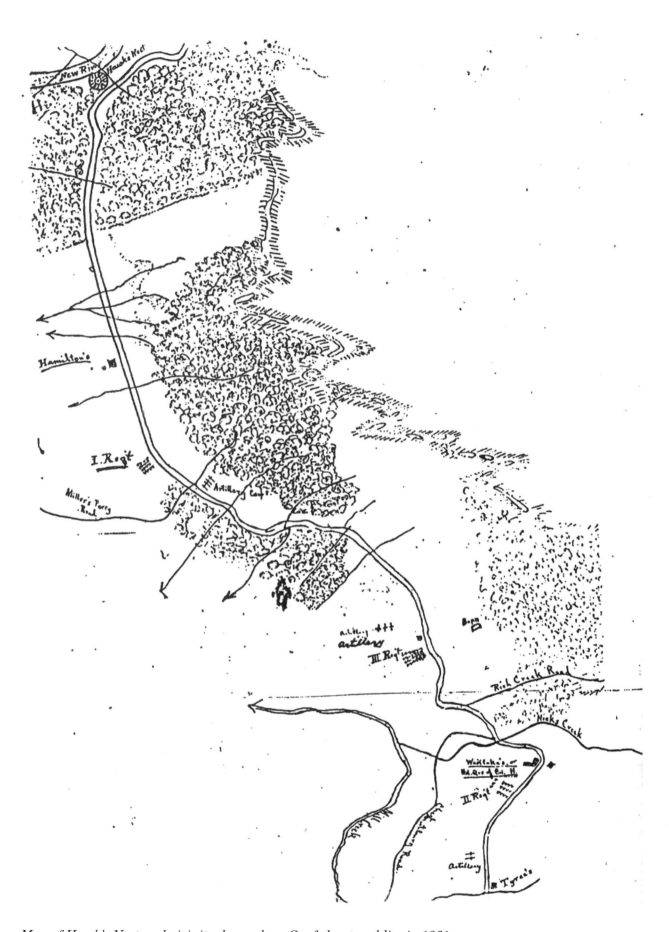

Map of Hawk's Nest and vicinity drawn by a Confederate soldier in 1861. VIRGINIA HISTORICAL SOCIETY

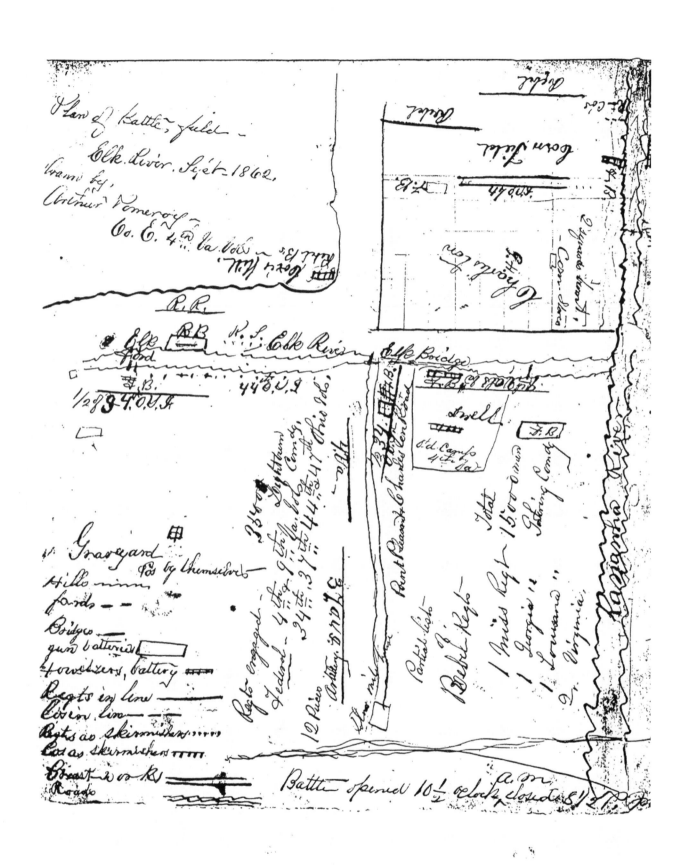

Map of the September 13, 1862, Battle of Charleston, Kanawha County. Drawn by Arthur Watts Pomeroy, Company E, 4th West Virginia Infantry. At the age of 18, Pomeroy enlisted July 16 or 22, 1861, at Mason City. LEWIS LEIGH JR. COLLECTION, U.S. ARMY MILITARY HISTORY INSTITUTE

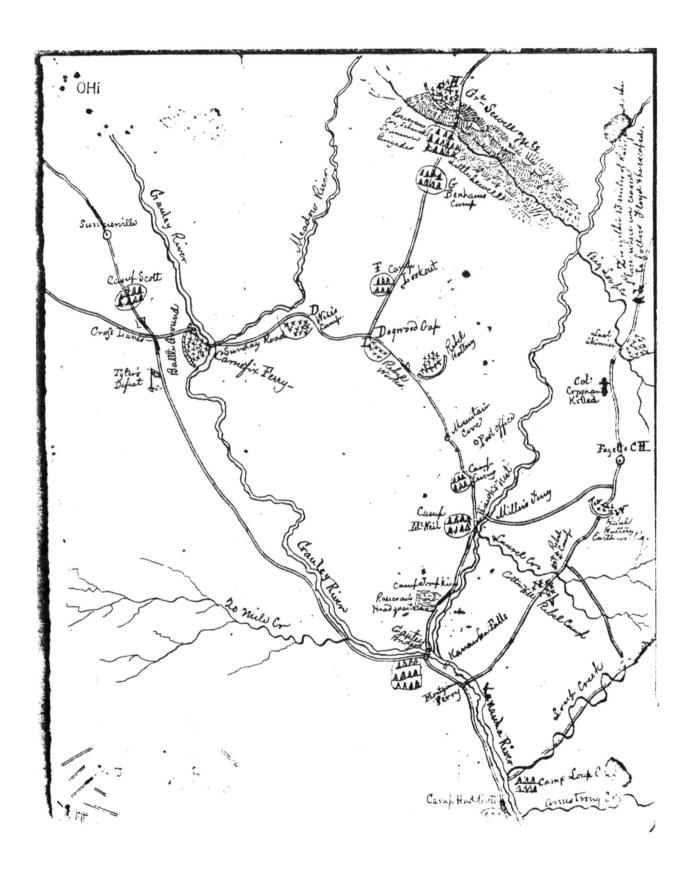

Map showing military camps between Gauley Bridge and Sewell Mountain in Fayette County. Drawn by Chaplain R.D. VanDuerson of the 12th O.V.I. OHIO HISTORICAL SOCIETY

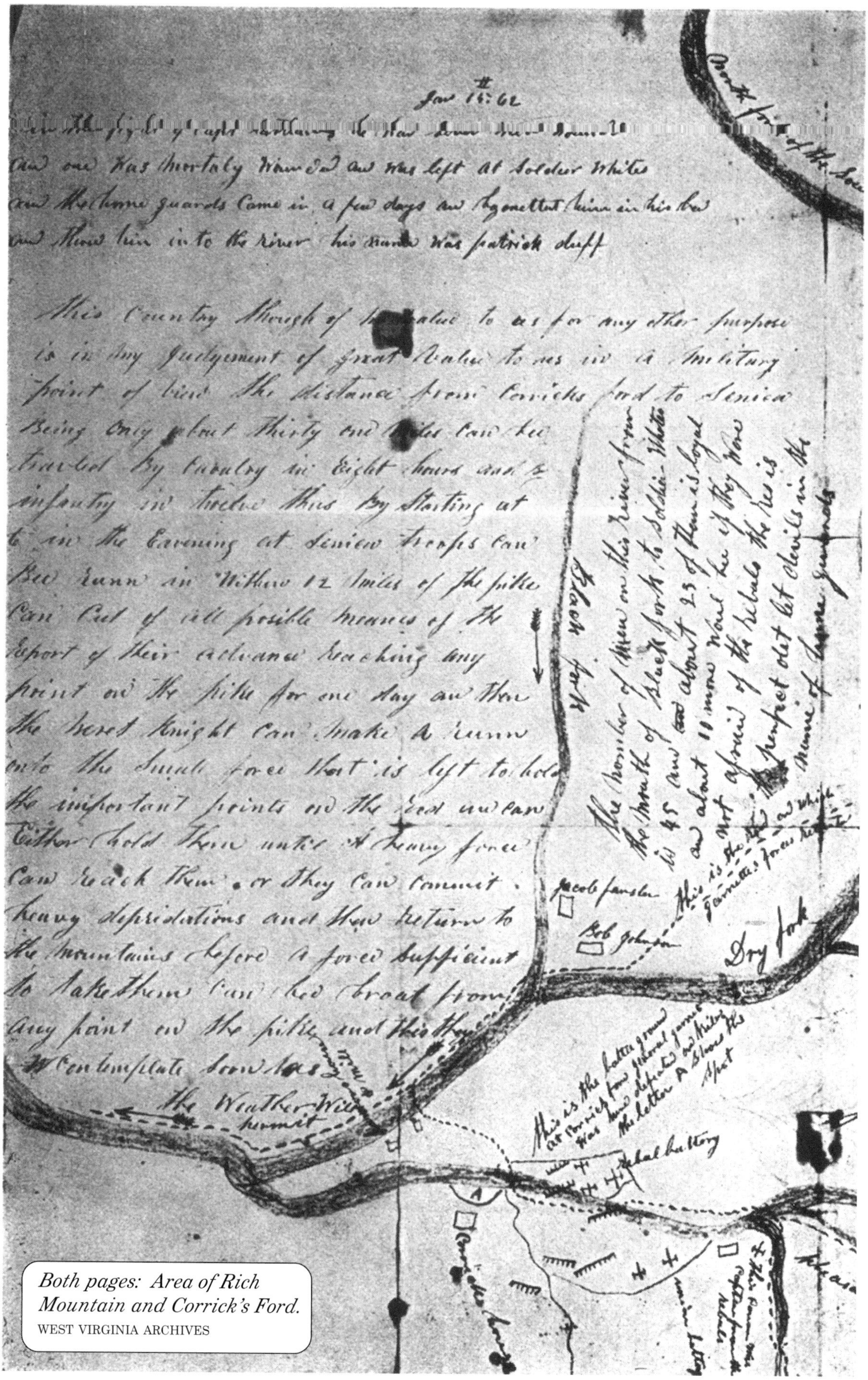
Jan 1st 62
and one was mortaly wounded and was left at Soldier White
and the home guards came in a few days and bayonetted him in his bed
and threw him into the river his name was patrick duff
This Country though of no value to us for any other purpose
is in my judgement of great value to us in a military
point of view the distance from Corricks ford to Senica
being only about thirty one miles can bee
traveled by cavalry in eight hours and by
infantry in twelve thus by starting at
6 in the evening at Senica troops can
bee runn in within 12 miles of the pike
can cut of all possible means of the
report of their advance reaching any
point on the pike for one day and then
the worst knight can make a runn
onto the small force that is left to hold
the important points on the pike and can
either hold them until a heavy force
can reach them or they can commit
heavy depredations and then return to
the mountains before a force sufficient
to take them can bee brought from
any point on the pike and this they
contemplate soon as
the weather will permit
Black fork
The number of men on this river from the mouth of Black fork to Soldier Whites is 45 and about 23 of them is loyal and about 10 more would be if they was not afraid of the rebels the rest is perfect old let devils in the name of home guards
This is the road white Garnett's forces retreated
Jacob Fansler
Bob Johnson
Dry fork
This is the battle ground at Corrick ford where general Garnett was defeated and killed A shows the spot
Rebel battery
A

Both pages: Area of Rich Mountain and Corrick's Ford.
WEST VIRGINIA ARCHIVES

Position of McClellan's advance on heights around Philippi. Sketch was made from the top of what is now Reservoir Hill above the athletic field of Alderson-Broaddus College. NEW YORK HISTORICAL SOCIETY

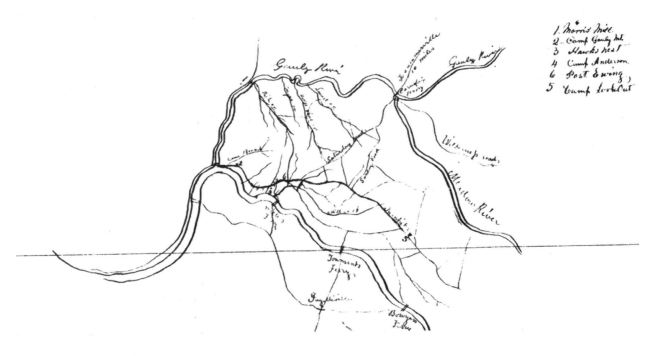

Fayette County area, possibly drawn by a soldier of the 34th Ohio Volunteer Infantry.
TERRY LOWRY COLLECTION

Magazine and Newspaper Sketch Artists

Some of the best known images of the Civil War were those recorded by the newspaper sketch artist. Almost all of them were featured in three New York magazines and newspapers: *Harper's Weekly*, *Frank Leslie's Illustrated Newspaper* and the *New York Illustrated News-*. There was also some coverage in the British *London Illustrated News.*

Many of the artists remain unknown, referred to in print only as our special correspondent or our special artist accompanying the troops, etc., while some became well known by name such as Alfred R. Waud. Many were soldiers themselves such as David Hunter Strother of *Harper's*, who wrote and drew under the pen name Porte Crayon, or the lesser-known John F.E. Hillen of the 34th Ohio Volunteer Infantry.

Unlike the photographers who had to rely on motionless subjects, the newspaper sketch artists could draw battle scenes, although they often tended to embellish them. Sometimes the artists were never present at the events they depicted and had to rely on their own imagination or a description by an eyewitness. Despite such flaws the newspaper sketch artist, whether civilian or soldier, provided a vast array of images of the war, including West Virginia. Sadly though, after the first year of the war interest in the West Virginia theater dwindled, except for the eastern panhandle and few images were sketched.

David Hunter Strother

Strother was born circa 1816 in Martinsburg, Berkeley County. He was a general in the Union army and fought in Virginia and Louisiana and with his cousin, Gen. David Hunter in the 1864 Virginia Valley campaign. Strother was well-known during and after the war as a correspondent and artist for *Harper's Weekly* magazine, using the pen name Porte Crayon. He died in 1888 and is buried in Berkeley Springs, Morgan County.

Alfred Rudolph Waud

Born in England circa 1828, Waud was the most prolific of the Civil War combat artists, although his West Virginia images are mostly of the eastern panhandle. He came to America in 1850 to work as an illustrator and at the outbreak of the war was a field artist "special" with the *New York Illustrated News* and in early 1862 joined *Harper's Weekly* for the remainder of the war and into the latter 1860s. He died of a heart attack while sketching the battlefields of Georgia in 1891.

The village of Clarksburg, Harrison County, 1861. FRANK LESLIE'S ILLUSTRATED NEWSPAPER, AUGUST 24, 1861

General Rosecrans, Commander of the Department of Western Virginia, and his staff at their headquarters in Clarksburg, 1861. FRANK LESLIE'S ILLUSTRATED NEWSPAPER, SEPTEMBER 21, 1861

Landing of Federal troops at Parkersburg, Wood County, May 27, 1861. A view from the south side of the Little Kanawha River. Note the one star of an Ohio Infantry unit atop the B&O Railroad depot, the Federal command post. FRANK LESLIES'S ILLUSTRATED NEWSPAPER, AUGUST 21, 1861

Parkersburg in 1861, viewed from the south side of the Little Kanawha river. LIBRARY OF CONGRESS

July 6, 1861 – Skirmish at Middle Fork bridge (Ellamore) near Beverly, Randolph County.
HARPER'S WEEKLY, AUGUST 3, 1861

Martinsburg, Berkeley County, during the war. HARPER'S WEEKLY, DECEMBER 3, 1864

Some 42 locomotive engines were destroyed by Gen "Stonewall" Jackson's Confederate soldiers at Martinsburg, Berkeley County, in June 1861. HARPER'S WEEKLY, AUGUST 3, 1861

Rebel troops arriving at and departing from Martinsburg, Berkeley County in early 1861.
HARPER'S WEEKLY, JUNE 29, 1861

This bridge was located on East Burke Street in Martinsburg.

RUINS OF THE VIADUCT, MARTINSBURG.

No. 8—Ruins of Colonade Bridge (B & O. R. R., Martinsburg, W. Va.
DESTROYED BY GENERAL STONEWALL JACKSON IN 1861

M S BURD

Baltimore & Ohio bridge at Grafton over the Tygrat River. THE NEW YORK ILLUSTRATED NEWSPPER

A panoramic view of Grafton, Taylor County, in 1861 when it was occupied by McClellan's troops. The Valley House, railroad machine house and Grafton House are to the left of the railroad bridge; to the right are the camps of the 15th and 16th Ohio Infantry Regiments.

FRANK LESLIE'S ILLUSTRATED NEWSPAPER, JUNE 29, 1861

DARING RIDE OF COL. LANDER AT THE BATTLE OF PHILIPPI.

THE intrepidity and daring courage of Col. Lander have often been the theme of conversation. His career has been full of that excitement which constant and secret danger creates, and the unceasing watchfulness necessary to guard against sudden surprises has made him at once cool in his recklessness and equal to any emergency. In the battle of Philippi his daring and his presence of mind were equally apparent. On reaching the brow of the hill overlooking Philippi, he beheld the enemy, and at the same moment observed the advancing column of Colonel Kelley. In a minute he had planted his cannon to play upon the camp of the Secessionists, and without thought of the danger, only thinking of the necessity of communicating with his brother officers, he put spurs to his horse and dashed down the face of the hill, the descent being at an angle of forty-five degrees. It was a perilous ride; and his soldiers gazed after him with hushed breath until they saw him reach the base in safety and dash across the town. A gallant soldier and fearless rider is Colonel Lander.

FRANK LESLIE'S ILLUSTRATED NEWSPAPER,
JUNE 29, 1861

The Battle of Philippi, Barbour County, June 4, 1861, between Federal troops under General Kelley and Confederate troops under General Porterfield, resulting in a Union victory. This was the first land battle of the war.
FRANK LESLIE'S ILLUSTRATED NEWSPAPER,
JUNE 22, 1861

Although this artist's sketch shows a well-organized battle on Main Street in Philippi, most accounts indicate the attack was a surprise skirmish between exhausted and poorly equipped forces on both sides. In spite of Porterfield's best efforts to rally his untrained troops, the overwrought rebels ran in uncontrollable panic, discarding their equipment and guns in their haste to escape. HARPER'S WEEKLY, JULY 6, 1861

HARPER'S WEEKLY, AUGUST 17, 1861

RETURN OF A FORAGING PARTY TO PHILIPPI.

OUR special artist writes: "While in Philippi I was attracted by an immense row in the street in front of the Court-house, and ran with the entire population of the town to learn the cause. Instead of the arrival of secession prisoners, or of an army courier, I found the tumult occasioned by the return from the country of a foraging party of volunteers—a squad of some half dozen, under command of a sergeant, with their spoil. Each man carried one or more young pigs—from the suckling up to the 'likely' shoat—and the squad entered the street in rank with piggy *shouldered* or *trailed*, according to the orders of the officer, to the vociferous music of their captives. As they neared the camp the town pigs took the alarm, and made a rush for the spoilers, followed by every cur of the neighborhood. The sergeant ordered 'double-quick,' but one old sow was too fast for the men; she broke their ranks and scattered them as they had routed the secessionists on the same ground. They saved their bacon by a rush into the Court-house yard."

THE BATTLE OF ROMNEY—SKIRMISH AT THE BRIDGE.—[SKETCHED BY MR. GOOKINS.]

Engagement at Romney, Hampshire County, June 11, 1861. These sketches by Mr. Gookins of the 11th Indiana show the 11th Indiana Zouaves crossing the bridge over the Potomac to attack the Confederates.
TOP: HARPER'S WEEKLY, JULY 6, 1861, BOTTOM: FRANK LESLIE'S ILLUSTRATED NEWSPAPER, JUNE 29, 1861

THE ENGAGEMENT AT ROMNEY, VA., JUNE 11th, 1861—THE ELEVENTH INDIANA ZOUAVES, COLONEL LEWIS WALLACE, CROSSING, ON THE DOUBLE QUICK, THE BRIDGE OVER THE POTOMAC.

THE DAY AFTER "ROMNEY."— THE ELEVENTH INDIANA ZOUAVES, COLONEL LEWIS WALLACE, IN CAMP McGINNIS, JUNE 12TH, 1861.

"The day after 'Romney' - The Eleventh Indiana Zouaves, Colonel Lewis Wallace, in Camp McGinnis, June 12th, 1861." FRANK LESLIE'S ILLUSTRATED NEWSPAPER, JUNE 29, 1861

Above, Wallace as a Major General. Left, Col. Lewis Wallace of the 11th Indiana Volunteers (Zouave Regiment) and his staff in West Virgina. Wallace would be known after the war for his famous novel Ben Hur.
FRANK LESLIE'S ILLUSTRATED NEWSPAPER, AUGUST 10, 1861

VIEW OF ROMNEY, VA. FROM A WAR-TIME SKETCH.

Brig. Gen. Kelley advanes upon Romney from New Creek Station. From a wartime sketch.

THE NEW YORK ILLUSTRATED NEWS, DECEMBER 28, 1861

GENERAL KELLEY'S FORCES MARCHING THROUGH MECHANICSBURG GAP, NEAR ROMNEY, WESTERN VIRGINIA. Sketched by E. Bott. See page 122.

"Gen. Kelly's troops crossing the Long Bridge, near Romney, on his retreat to Cumberland, Va. Sketched by our Special Artist." THE NEW YORK ILLUSTRATED NEWS

"The evacuation of Romney. Federal troops passing up the principal street on their way to Cumberland, Va. From a sketch by our Special Artist." THE NEW YORK ILLUSTRATED NEWS, FEBRUARY 8, 1862

NEW YORK
ILLUSTRATED NEWS.

No. 110.—Vol. V.　　NEW-YORK, MONDAY, DECEMBER 9, 1861.　　Price Six Cents.

OPEN THIS PAPER WITH CARE BEFORE YOU CUT IT.

1. JACOB FLANAGAN.　2. WILLIAM ROBINSON.　3. WILLIAM NELSON.　4. DANIEL RORABUGH.　5. WILLIAM SHEFORAH.
BUSHWHACKER PRISONERS AT ROMNEY, VA. Sketched from Life by E. Bott. Page 90.

First Virginia Camp   Court House   Valley Bank of Virginia   Hospital

Top: "First half of the sketch entitled 'View of Romney, West Virginia, in possession of General Kelley when threatened by a strong force of Confederates' sketched by A.M. Bott." Bottom: Second half of Bott's sketch. THE NEW YORK ILLUSTRATED NEWS, FEBRUARY 1, 1862

7th Virginia and Detachment   Ohio 5th and 8th   Capt. Ringgold's Cavalry   Hospital
   of 3d Virginia Camps   Encampments

Belington and Camp Laurel Hill, Barbour County, showing the fortified Confederate camp and batteries.
FRANK LESLIE'S ILLUSTRATED NEWSPAPER, AUGUST 17, 1861.

The engagement at Belington between Ohio and Indiana regiments and a detachment of Georgia troops.
FRANK LESLIE'S ILLUSTRATED NEWSPAPER, JULY 20, 1861.

*Skirmish near Laurel Hill.
Effect of a shell among the
rebel dragoons.*
THE NEW YORK ILLUSTRATED
NEWS, JULY 22, 1861

*Mis-titled as the death of Confederate Gen. Robert Garnett at the Battle of Laurel Hill. Actually, Garnett
was killed in the fight at Corrick's Ford (Parsons), Tucker County. Sketched for* Harper's Weekly,
August 3, 1861, by C.R. HARPER'S WEEKLY, AUGUST 3, 1861.

THE DEATH OF THE REBEL GENERAL GARNETT, AT THE BATTLE OF LAUREL HILL.—[SEE PAGE 484.]

No. 164.—THE BATTLE OF RICH MOUNTAIN, BETWEEN THE U. S. FORCES UNDER COL. ROSENCRANZ, OF MAJOR M'CLELLAN'S COMMAND, AND THE REBELS UNDER COLONEL PEGRAM—RETREAT OF THE REBELS.

On July 11, 1861, Federal troops, under the command of General McClellan, routed the Confederates holding the pass over Rich Mountain, near Beverly, Randolph County. This victory gave the Union control of much of northwestern Virginia. This battle allowed the western counties to form the present state of West Virginia. FRANK LESLIE'S ILLUSTRATED NEWSPAPER, JULY 27, 1861.

ADVANCE OF GENERAL ROSECRANS'S DIVISION THROUGH THE FORESTS, TO ATTACK THE CONFEDERATES AT RICH MOUNTAIN

FRANK LESLIE'S ILLUSTRATED NEWSPAPER, AUGUST 31, 1861.

Battle of Rich Mountain, Randolph County, between the division of Major-General McClellan's command, let by General Rosecrans, and the rebel troops under Colonel Pegram, July 11, 1861.
TOP: HARPER'S WEEKLY, JULY 27, 1861, BOTTOM: FRANK LESLIE'S ILLUSTRATED NEWSPAPER, JULY 27, 1861

Brig. Gen. William S. Rosecrans, commanding the Federal army in western Virginia.

The Battle of Rich Mountain from an original lithograph.
PICTORIAL HISTORIES COLLECTION

THE BURIAL OF THE INDIANA VOLUNTEERS WHO FELL IN THE BATTLE OF RICH MOUNTAIN.

Two views of the Battle of Rich Mountain. FRANK LESLIE'S ILLUSTRATED NEWSPAPER, TOP: AUGUST 10, 1861, BOTTOM JULY 20, 1861

THE WAR IN WESTERN VIRGINIA—BATTLE AT CORRICK'S FORD, BETWEEN THE TROOPS OF GEN. McCLELLAN'S COMMAND, LED BY GEN. MORRIS, AND THE REBEL ARMY UNDER GEN. GARNETT, ON SATURDAY, JULY 13, 1861.
FROM A SKETCH BY OUR SPECIAL ARTIST ACCOMPANYING MAJOR-GENERAL McCLELLAN'S COMMAND.—See Page 179.

Battle of Corrick's Ford (Parsons), Tucker County, July 13, 1861. Gen. Garnett was the first Confederate general to be killed in battle during the war. BOTH: FRANK LESLIE'S ILLUSTRATED NEWSPAPER, AUGUST 3, 1861

Cheat River.   Dead Georgian Volunteer.   Colonel Dumont.   Major Gordon, who closed General Garnett's eyes.

No, 166.—BATTLE OF CORRACK'S FORD—DISCOVERY OF THE BODY OF GENERAL GARNETT, BY MAJOR GORDON AND COLONEL DUMONT, AFTER THE BATTLE.

Ohio Volunteers crossing the mountains into West Virginia. Drawn by James Beard.
THE NEW YORK ILLUSTRATED NEWS, JULY 22, 1861

"The Secessionist Army - Irregular Riflemen of the Alleghenies, Va." A vivid portrayal of irregulars, partisans or guerilla fighters for the South in the mountains of West Virginia. HARPER'S WEEKLY, JULY 20, 1861

No. 201.—PRISONERS CAPTURED BY MAJOR-GENERAL McCLELLAN'S COLUMN IN WESTERN VIRGINIA, UNDER GUARD AT BEVERLY, RANDOLPH COUNTY, VA.—(SEE PAGE 94.)

Confederate prisoners captured in the early West Virginia campaigns, under guard in Beverly, Randolph County. FRANK LESLIE'S ILLUSTRATED NEWSPAPER, AUGUST 17, 1861

Tray Run Viaduct on the mainline of the Baltimore & Ohio Railroad near Rowlesburg, Preston County. This was one of the most important sections of the railroad and was heavily guarded by Union troops throughout the war. FRANK LESLIE'S ILLUSTRATED NEWSPAPER, AUGUST 3, 1861

THE SIXTEENTH REGIMENT, OHIO VOLUNTEERS, COLONEL IRWINE, CROSSING THE TRAY RUN VIADUCT NEAR CHEAT RIVER ON THE BALTIMORE AND OHIO RAILROAD

ROWLESBURG, THE HEAD-QUARTERS OF GENERAL HILL, IN WESTERN VIRGINIA.—[SEE PAGE 487.]

Rowlesburg, PrestonCounty, headquarters of General Hill in western Virginia.
HARPERS'S WEEKLY, AUGUST 3, 1861

Drawing by a member of the 7th O.V.I. of part of the camp of Col. Erastus B. Tyler's 7th Ohio Volunteer Infantry at Kessler's Cross Lanes, Nicholas County, August 1861. HARPERS'S WEEKLY, SEPTEMBER 14, 1861

Prior to the war, artist Frank Beard and James Beard were involved in the lithography business in New York with John F.E. Hillen. The Beards enlisted in Neff's Detachment, Cincinnati Volunteer Rifle Company.

THE NEW YORK ILLUSTRATED NEWS, SEPTEMBER 16, 1861

Belle Air, Ohio – steamboats conveying troops and munitions for the Federal forces on the Great Kanawha.

FRANK LESLIE'S ILLUSTRATED NEWSPAPER, AUGUST 17, 1861

ARREST OF A SECESSION SPY BY A GUARD
OF THE OHIO SEVENTH.
SKETCHED BY FRANK BEARD.—Page 816.

Our correspondent writes:

This sketch shows a little incident which took place on the 18th inst. The picket guard arresting a rebel spy. As I luckily was a witness I can send you a correct sketch. The guard halted him, but he only quickened his pace from a trot to a gallop. He was instantly surrounded by our agile men and taken. This is an every day occurrence and will serve to show your readers how the thing is done.

FRANK BEARD.

FELLE AIR, OHIO—STEAMBOATS CONVEYING TROOPS AND MUNITIONS OF WAR FOR THE FEDERAL FORCES ON THE GREAT KANAWHA.—From a Sketch by Capt. Robert, Wheeling, Va.—See Page 211.

THE NEW YORK ILLUSTRATED NEWS,
SEPTEMBER 16, 1861

Gallant charge by Col. Piatt's Mounted Zouaves, attached to the 34th Ohio Volunteer Infantry, on Jenkins' Rebel Cavalry, in the pass called "Devil's Elbow," Cabell County, western Virginia. Sketched by Ensign J.F.E. Hillen. THE NEW YORK ILLUSTRATED NEWS, DECEMBER 28, 1861

Sutton, Braxton County, 1861.

John Francis Edward Hillen

John F.E. Hillen was born circa 1821 in Brussels, Belgium, and married Isabella Johnson September 14, 1847, in New York where he worked as a lithographer with Frank and James Beard. He enlisted as a private in Company F, 34th Ohio Volunteer Infantry at Camp Lucas, Ohio, July 25, 1861. He was appointed regimental color sergeant August 1, 1861, and on January 24, 1862, was detached to return to Ohio to recruit. He joined the Permanent Party at the Depot for Ohio Volunteer Recruiting Service at Cincinnati January 27, 1862. By July 1862 he was listed as "on duty Secy" and in August and September as "on duty mapper at Hqr." October 16, 1862, at the hospital at Gallipolis, Ohio, he was given a medical discharge stating, "Since November 1st, 1861, when the regiment was at Mud Bridge said Private Hillen has been severely afflicted with asthma, shortness of breath, so much so that he has not been able to march with his company at any time. He has not been reported for duty since November 1st, 1861 . . . asthma, shortness of breath, pain in the breast, chronic diarrhea and general disability. He is . . . totally unfit for a soldier."

Hillen's discharge stated that when he entered military service he was a lithographer, and a number of his wartime drawings ran in *The New York Illustrated News* and *Harper's Weekly.*

Hillen died August 12, 1865, at New York of "asthmatic disease" and is buried at Cypress Hills Cemetery, New York.

Pioneer Company of the 34th Ohio Volunteer Infantry (Piatt's Zouaves) constructing a raft bridge over Twenty Pole Creek in western Virginia, near the Kentucky line in the face of a superior number of the Rebels. Sketched for The New York Illustrated News *by Ensign (color sergeant) John F.E. Hillen, Company F, 34th O.V.I.* THE NEW YORK ILLUSTRATED NEWS

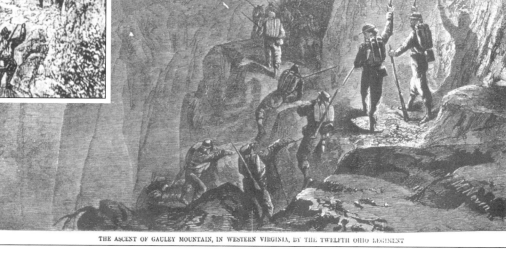

THE ASCENT OF GAULEY MOUNTAIN, IN WESTERN VIRGINIA, BY THE TWELFTH OHIO REGIMENT

Two different views of the mountainous terrain between Gauley Bridge and Sewell Mountain. This terrain precluded the easy movement of troops by both sides. BOTH HARPER'S WEEKLY, OCTOBER 5, 1861

View of the mountain region in western Virginia, from the summit of Limestone Mountain, Tucker County. HARPER'S WEEKLY, NOVEMBER 23, 1861

William L. Johnson, who fought with the militia at Barboursville, recounted after the war the story of two members of the 34th Ohio who were killed while the regiment was stationed in Cabell County.

"Two zouaves and Bill Collins were murdered, on Beech Fork . . . Robert Mays and I were on Robert Adkin's farm, and heard the bushwhackers halt these men. Collins lived on Madison Creek. Eight or nine of us crossed the hill, and saw two of them dead and the third man wounded. When we got in sight, and saw the bushwhackers dressed in blue uniforms which they had taken from the Zouaves, George saw that we were about to shoot at him and his companions, and he said Boys, don't shoot; these are our boys.

"We went on, and saw the wounded man, and they said they had sent two more to head-quarters. Robert Mays was displeased and said he wanted them buried right, and the bushwhackers agreed to let all the men there look at them. We found them buried behind a root and covered up with leaves and chunks. We then buried them, in the same place, a little better, and came on down and found a wounded man guarded under a beech tree.

"We started from there, and they said they were going to take him to headquarters. He wa a zouave. . . . We passed on two hundred yards, and I heard gun fire. I started home and met the guards of the wounded man without their prisoner. . . ."

BDER OF TWO OF PIATT'S ZOUAVES, 34TH OHIO, BY EIGHT OF THE REBEL CHIVALRY, ON BEECH FORK, CABEL COUNTY, WESTERN VIRGINIA. Sketched by Ensign J. F. C. Hillan, Piatt's Zouaves. See page 250.

JOHN SNIDER, A FEDERAL SCOUT ATTACHED TO GENERAL KELLY'S COMMAND IN WESTERN VIRGINIA. Sketched from Life by E. Bott. See page 90.

THE NEW YORK ILLUSTRATED NEWS, DECEMBER 9, 1861

Western Virginia home guards.
THE NEW YORK ILLUSTRATED NEWS,
JANUARY 18, 1862

*Mail call at General McCellan's
headquarters at Webster, Taylor
County, summer of 1861. This
house was also the birthplace of
Anna Jarvis, the founder of
Mother's Day. Webster was an
important depot for both troops
and supplies. Present-day Route
250 in front of the house connected
Wheeling and Staunton. The
house is operated by Thunder on
the Tygart Inc., a non-profit
foundation founded in 1994.*
U.S. ARMY MILITARY HISTORY INSTITUTE,
MASSACHUSETTS COMMANDERY, MILITARY
ORDER OF THE LOYAL LEGION

SURPRISE OF REBELS BETWEEN HURRICANE AND LOGAN, WESTERN VIRGINIA, BY A DETACHMENT OF COLONEL PIATT'S ZOUAVES (THIRTY-FOURTH OHIO VOLUNTEER UNDER LIEUTENANT ROWE.—[Sketched by Sergeant Hillen.]

HARPER'S WEEKLY, JANUARY 18,1862

THE NEW YORK ILLUSTRATED NEWS, JANUARY 25,1862

GOVERNOR PIERPONT'S STORE-ROOM, WHEELING, VA., CONTAINING STORES FOR TEN VIRGINIA REGIMENTS. Sketched by E. M. Bott.

North Mountain is in Berkeley County, near Hedgesville. Drawn by Lucian Gray, 1st (West) Virginia Volunteer Infantry.
PICTORIAL HISTORIES PUBLISHING

Winter quarters (1861-62) of the 12th Ohio Volunteer Infantry, one mile south of Charleston, Kanawha County on the Kanawha River. Legend: (A) Colonel's quarters with a guard in front; (B) Guard-house with a guard in front; (C) Commissary; (D) Stable; (E) Abandoned salt works; (F) House where Gen. Albert Gallatin Jenkins of the Confederate cavalry lived. Sketched by Harry Kramer (possibly Henry Kramer of the 12th O.V.I.) THE NEW YORK ILLUSTRATED NEWS, MAY 10, 1862

CHARLESTOWN, VA., NOW IN POSSESSION OF GEN. BANKS.—Page 356.

Charlestown is the first important post south of the Potomac occupied by the advance of Gen. Banks. The drawing is made by our special artist Mr. Lumley, who is with the advance guard of this division of the Grand Army of the Potomac. The town is situated on the road from Harper's Ferry to Winchester, to the west of the Blue Ridge.

Charlestown, Jefferson County, while in possession of Gen. Nathaniel Banks and his Federal troops in 1862. Sketched by a "Mr. Lumley," a special artist with the advance guard of the division of the Army of the Potomac. THE NEW YORK ILLUSTRATED NEWS, APRIL 12, 1862

"Charlestown, Virginia, from the tower of the Expicopal Church now used as a signal station by the National Troops. From a sketch by our special artist, F.H. Schell." FRANK LESLIE'S ILLUSTRATED NEWSPAPER, NOVEMBER 8, 1862

The Philadelphia Corn Exchange Regiment, fording the Potomac River near Shepherdstown, Jefferson County. Sketched by Alfred R. Waud. HARPER'S WEEKLY, OCTOBER 11, 1862

Two views, artists's original and final sketch, showing the 5th New York at Pack Horse Ford, September 19, 1862. They are firing from the C&O Canal on the Maryland side towards the cement mill across the Potomac River on the West Virginia side. TOP: HARPER'S WEEKLY, OCTOBER 11, 1862. BOTTOM: LIBRARY OF CONGRESS

An attempt at newspaper humor attacking the military. Note the center racist cartoon of "Wheeling, Virginia." THE NEW YORK ILLUSTRATED NEWS, MAY 31, 1862

JOHN W. PACKHAM, THE YOUNGEST CORPORAL IN THE ARMY.

JOHN W. PACKHAM,

Fifer and Regimental Marker to the 34th Regt. Ohio Zouaves.

As we make no difference between the Commander-in-Chief and the drummer-boy, but are ever ready to celebrate valor, we have great pleasure in publishing the portrait of a noble little hero. The following letter relates the event:

POINT PLEASANT, VA., }
October 10th, 1862. }

SIR—As you are one of the very few editors who take notice of bravery in privates in our army during this dreadful war, I send you the likeness of the "Little Hero of Co. F, 34th regiment, Ohio Zouaves," aged 13 years. It was taken three months previous to the following incident—while he was on furlough, he being regularly enlisted in the beginning of the war.

[Nov. 8, 1862.

At the late battle of Fayetteville, Va., John W. Packham, fifer and regimental marker, son of Lieut. A. Packham, of the 34th regiment, Ohio Zouaves, was with the ambulances, and about 1,000 yards in advance of the regiment; they were halted by 2,000 rebels, across a dry creek bottom, about 50 yards from the road; some 50 advanced from the cover of the woods, and called out (Johnny being the only one in the train who was in uniform), "You —— little redtop devil, come over here, or I'll kill you." He answered, "No; I can't do that." Again they called; again he answered "No." Another rebel now advanced a few paces, and said, "You —— little fool, we won't hurt you, if you come over; we only want to talk to you." The little hero answered, "I know what you want—I can't come." The rebel took aim and fired, wounding the little fellow in the centre of the right knee. He fell, and lay between the contending parties during three hours' hard fighting, for that one shot brought on the engagement in the rear. He was finally brought off the field by E. Roberts, private, Co. F, amid a shower of bullets, without further harm to his person, but having six large bullet holes through the back of his jacket.

Upon being asked why he did not go over to the rebels and save himself, the little hero said, "Because they wanted me to tell them how many soldiers we had got!" Yours obediently,

JUSTICE.

P. S.—We had only the 34th and 37th regiments, Ohio, and six small pieces artillery, manned and served by the same, against the rebel Gen. Loring's 8,000.

J. W. PACKHAM, FIFER AND REGIMENTAL MARKER OF 34TH OHIO ZOUAVES. FROM A PHOTOGRAPH BY BALL & THOMAS, CINCINNATI.

Harper's Weekly *and* Frank Leslie's Illustrated Newspaper *both published a story and picture of John W. Packham, 34th Ohio Volunteer Infantry, the boy hero of the battle of Fayetteville, Fayette County, September 10, 1862. Note* Leslie's *sketch is more detailed; the artist apparently used the original photo as a model. Unlike* Harper's, *Packham has a fife in his right hand, and his left hand is different. In* Harper's *he is clearly resting on a chair. These two versions illustrate the alterations and embellishments the sketch artists often utilized.* TOP: HARPER'S WEEKLY, NOVEMBER 5, 1862. BOTTOM: FRANK LESLIE'S ILLUSTRATED NEWSPAPER, NOVEMBER 8, 1862

Governor Pierpont welcomes the arrival of Illinois troops to the soil of Virginia in front of the customhouse in Wheeling. THE NEW YORK ILLUSTRATED NEWS, AUGUST 12, 1861

FRANK LESLIE'S ILLUSTRATED NEWSPAPER, AUGUST 3, 1862

SCOUTING PARTY OF THE NINTH INDIANA VOLUNTEERS, COLONEL MILROY—CALLED "THE TIGERS OF THE BLOODY NINTH."

FIGHT OF DUFFIE'S CAVALRY, NEAR HUNTER'S HOUSE, CHARLESTOWN, VA., COVERING THE RETREAT OF THE FEDERAL FORCES.

GALLANT CHARGE OF THE SIXTH MICHIGAN CAVALRY OVER THE CONFEDERATE BREASTWORKS, NEAR FALLING WATERS, JULY 14TH, 1863.

Harpers Ferry, Virginia Batteries in the foreground. One of three sketches from The New York Illustrated News, *June 1, 1861. It shows the Potomac River bridge and arsenal before their destruction.*
HARPERS FERRY NATIONAL HISTORICAL PARK HF-342

This view is of present-day High Steet which runs from Bolivar down to the center of Harpers Ferry.
NEW YORK ILLUSTRATED NEWS

"General Banks's Division recrossing the Potomac from Williamsport, MD., to attack the Confederate Army under General Jackson. The band of the Forty-sixth Pennsylvania Volunteers plays the national airs on the [West] Virginia shore." HARPER'S WEEKLY

BURNING OF THE UNITED STATES ARSENAL AT HARPER'S FERRY. VA. APRIL 18TH. 1861.

FRANK LESLIE'S ILLUSTRATED NEWSPAPER

A rebel battery overlooking Harpers Ferry. FRANK LESLIE'S ILLUSTRATED NEWSPAPER, JUNE 1, 1862

SECESSION BATTERY AT HARPER'S FERRY ERECTED ON THE HEIGHT OVERLOOKING THE TOWN AND COMMANDING THE RAILROAD BRIDGE, CANAL, ETC.

Harpers Ferry view from Jefferson Rock as pictured in the July 6, 1861 issue of Harper's Weekly.

General view of Harper's Ferry and the Maryland Heights from Harper's History of the Great Rebellion published in 1876.

This drawing of Harpers Ferry in the summer of 1861 appeared in a French magazine.
HARPERS FERRY NATIONAL HISTORICAL PARK HP-439

Captain Owen's Rhode Island Battery of Burnside's Corps, on Bolivar Heights, commanding the roads to Charlestown. THE NEW YORK ILLUSTRATED NEWS, NOVEMBER 8, 1862

Earthworks extending across Camp Hill, guarding the road from Harpers Ferry to Charlestown and Winchester. THE NEW YORK ILLUSTRATED NEWS, OCTOBER 25, 1862

Two members of the Ninth New York Regiment take down the rebel flag at Harpers Ferry, probably in 1861. HARPER'S WEEKLY, AUGUST 3, 1862

This Harper's Weekly *drawing was actually in the magazine after 1876, so it may or may not have been drawn during the war. The soldier's graveyard at Bolivar Heights, near Harpers Ferry, Loudon Heights on the right and Maryland Heights on the left in the distance.*
HARPERS FERRY NATIONAL HISTORICAL PARK HF-459

Encampment of Union troops on the summit of Camp Hill with Harpers Ferry and Maryland Heights in the distance. Sketched by L.M. Hamilton.
THE NEW YORK ILLUSTRATED NEWS

This was General Stevenson's Union army headquarters. This was sketched by noted combat artist Alfred R. Waud, probably for Harper's Weekly.

"Campaign in Virginia—A street in Harper's Ferry during the passage of the Potomac by the National troops from Maryland, Oct. 24, 1862.—sketched by our special artist."
FRANK LESLIE'S ILLUSTRATED NEWS, NOVEMBER 15, 1862

"Campaign in Virginia—General Geary's division crossing the Shenandoah from Harper's Ferry to take possession of Loudon Heights.—sketched by our special artist."
FRANK LESLIE'S ILLUSTRATED NEWSPAPER, NOVEMBER 15, 1862

"Campaign in Virginia—The reconnaissance to Charlestown—scene at the railroad station—chivalrous behavior of Sesech lady.—sketched by our special artist."
FRANK LESLIE'S ILLUSTRATED NEWSPAPER, NOVEMBER 15, 1862

Civilian

Art

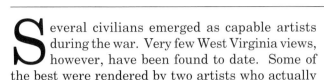

Several civilians emerged as capable artists during the war. Very few West Virginia views, however, have been found to date. Some of the best were rendered by two artists who actually witnessed the events. One is of a skirmish near Buffalo, Putnam County, and the other is of an encampment at Charleston, Kanawha County.

Joseph Hubert Diss Debar

Joseph H. Diss Debar was born in Strasbourg, France on March 6, 1817 and received a classical education in some of Europe's best schools. He learned French, German, English and became proficient in Latin and Greek. In 1842 he moved to the United States, first to Boston, then to Cincinnati, Ohio, where he married, and then to Parkersburg, Wood County.

Diss Debar developed an interest in western Virginia lands and served as an agent for 10,000 acres in Doddridge County, which he colonized with families from outside the area. The colony was named Saint Clara in honor of his wife.

In 1863 he came to Wheeling as the duly elected delegate from Doddridge County, but his election was contested by Ephriam Bee. While awaiting the outcome he drew numerous pictures, including the governor and delegates. Peter Van Winkle of Wood County approached him to draw a state seal for the new state of West Virginia.

Diss Bebar was elected to the state legislature and with his artistic talents sketched many portraits and events of his time. As a legislator he helped pass the Bill for the Encouragement of Foreign Immigration. In 1864 Gov. Arthur Boreman appointed him Commissioner of Immigrants for the new state. He held office until 1872. In 1870 he published the *West Virginia Handbook and Immigrant's Guide,* and he also was influential in the settlement of the community of Helvetia in Randolph County. In 1876 he left West Virginia and moved to Philadelphia, Pennsylvania where he reportedly got involved with psychics and mediums. He died in 1905.

WEST VIRGINIA STATE ARCHIVES

The following five pages are drawings of Joseph H. Diss Debar.

WEST VIRGINIA STATE ARCHIVES

Diss Debar sketched Thomas Jonathan, later "Stonewall," Jackson on his 1860 visit to the Mineral Wells Hotel near Parkersburg. There is some question as to whether Jackson was born in Clarksburg or Parkersburg in 1834.

Union soldiers.

Peter Van Winkle of Wood County with President Abraham Lincoln, sketched in 1864.

A squard of citizen home guards scouting for guerrillas and horse thieves during the Civil War.

Capt. Daniel Dusky (behind bars), a notorious guerrilla leader with the Moccasin Rangers, was captured in the Little Kanawha Valley by Bass' "Snake Hunters" and sent to the military guardhouse at

Parkersburg. He was forwarded to Atheneum Prison in Wheeling to be tried by the Federal court. He knew A.I. Boreman and requested a meeting with him, illustrated here. Dusky promised to stop the guerrilla activity in the valley if he were released, but Boreman, a guerrilla hater, refused to listen to his plan.

Old neighbors meet after the war. Sketch done in 1865.

The New York Times *on June 2, 1860, published the "View of Wheeling." The description of the industrial city stated the sky was not canopied with smoke as it was in Pittsburgh, but there was enough shiny soot to darken brick buildings, damage furniture and blacken carpets.*

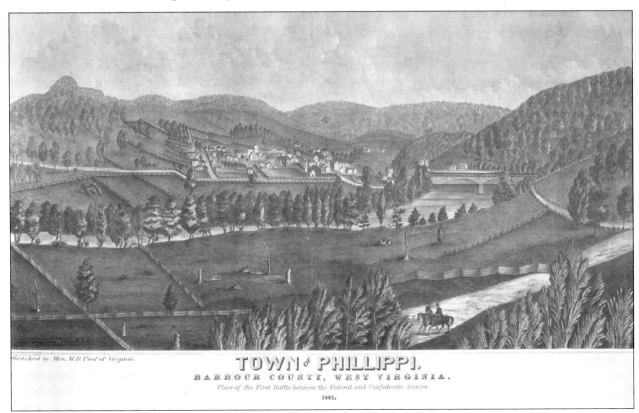

Sketched by Mrs. M.D. Paul of Virginia.

TOWN of PHILLIPPI.
BARBOUR COUNTY, WEST VIRGINIA.
Place of the First Battle between the Federal and Confederate Armies.
1861.

An English Lord and a Rebel Captain.

Pryce Lewis, a Union spy employed by Alan Pinkerton, spent time in the Kanawha Valley prior to the Scary Creek battle, obtaining information on Confederate troops and their fortification. He posed as an English tourist and was befriended by Colonel Patton and Col. Christopher Q. Tompkins, but was rebuffed by Gen. Henry A. Wise when he tried to get a pass to travel to Richmond. Although he eventually made it back to Union lines in Ohio, he was too late to give any useful information to Gen. Jacob D. Cox, who had already fought at Scary Creek. Lewis, glass in had, toasts Col. George S. Patton during their meeting at the Valcoulon Mansion, Camp Tompkins. Sam Bridgeman, Lewis' assistant and traveling companion, looks on from the left. ALAN PINKERTON'S *SPY OF THE REBELLION*

This rather idyllic scene of Charleston, Kanawha County, was painted in 1863 by Margaretta Doddridge, from a vantage point near what is now Morris Street. It shows a Union army camp (Camp White) on the south side of the Kanawha River, around the Ferry Branch outlet just downriver from the present C&O station. PICTORIAL HISTORIES COLLECTION

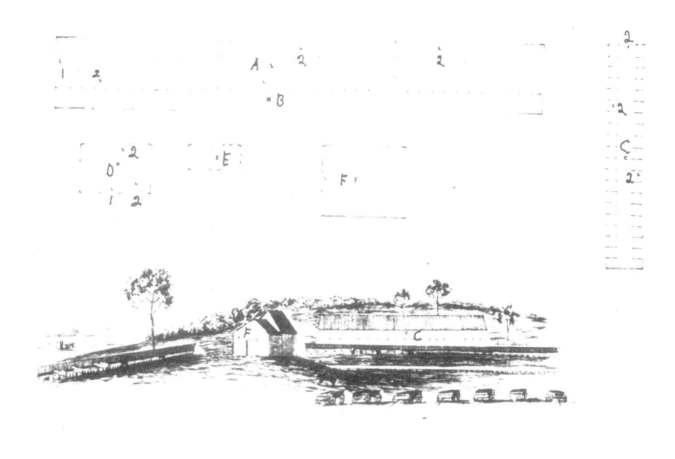

THE CORRAL ᴀᴛ PARKERSBERG W. Vₐ.

REFERENCE

U.S. corral at Parkersburg, West Virginia: A) main building; B) shed; C) building Nᵒ· 2; D) building Nᵒ· 3; E) office; F) feed house; G) feed rack; H) watering trough; I) feed trough: 1) door; 2) stalls. Scale: one inch equals ten feet. By F.B. Ladd, 1865. NATIONAL ARCHIVES

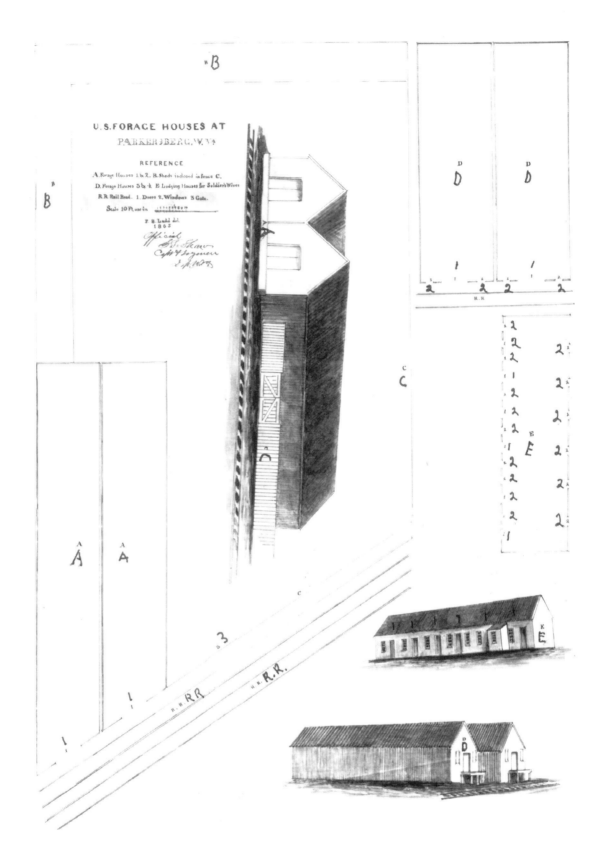

U.S. forage houses at Parkersburg, West Virginia: A) forage houses 1 & 2; B) sheds inclosed in fence; C&D) forage houses 3&4; E) lodging houses for soldiers; wives; RR) railroad; 1) doors; 2) windows; 3) gate. Scale: one inch equals ten feet. By F.B. Ladd, 1865. The location of these building has not yet been determined. There is a reference to the yardmaster on Depot Street buying animal forage for the Army, and they may have been located there. NATIONAL ARCHIVES

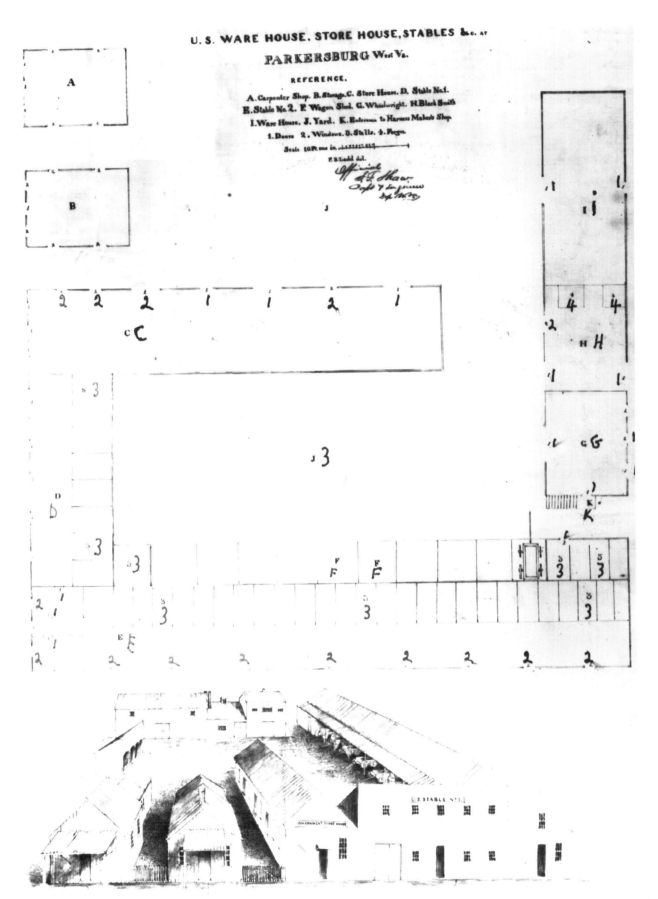

U.S. ware house, store house, stables, &c at Parkersburg, West Virginia: A) carpenter shop; B) storage; C) store house; D) stable No. 1; E) stable No. 2; F) wagon shed; G) wheelwright; H) black smith; I) ware house; J) yard; K) entrance to Harness maker's shop; 1) doors; 2) windows; 3) stalls; 4) forges. Scale: one inch equals ten feet. By F.B. Ladd, 1865. The location of these buildings is unknown.

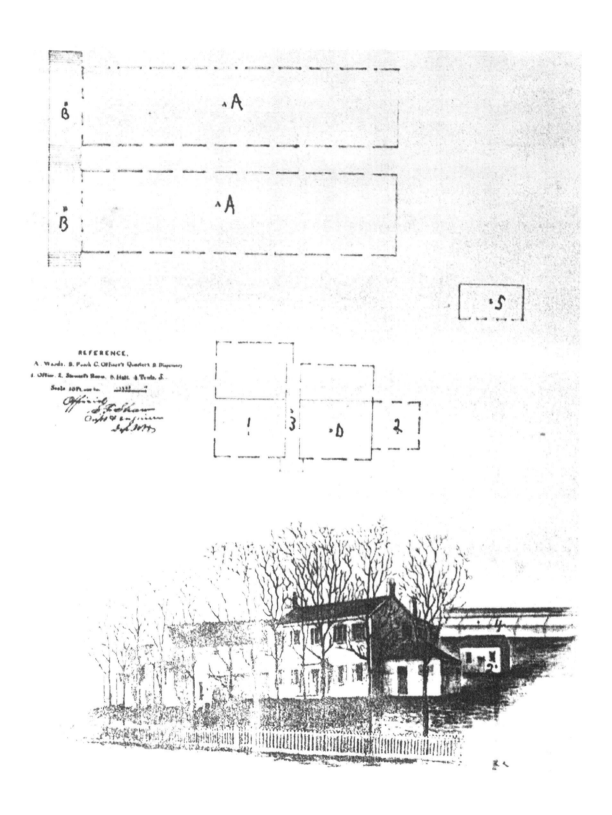

One of the U.S. Army's hospitals was operated in a two-story brick house on the northeast corner of Fourth and Avery Streets owned by Henry Logan. This sketch by an anonymous government artist was done in 1865. A) wards; B) porch; C) officers' quarters; D) dispensary; 1) office; 2) stewart's room; 3) hall; 4) tents; 5) (blank). NATIONAL ARCHIVES

"One fall the Rebels came into the Valley and established a camp on the farm below ours and another on the farm above. They had been in camp there for several weeks when a Federal army crossed the Ohio, came up the Valley before daylight and began firing on the pickets at the lower camp. The Rebels moved up the Valley in wild confusion to the camp above, where they rallied somewhat and sent a small company of cavalry down the road to check the Federals. About this time my father, growing curious about the situation, walked out to the turnpike, which is a hundred yards or so from the house. All the rest of us were content to watch the proceedings out of the windows. Just then the Rebel cavalrymen were fired upon by the Federals, and back they came with bullets flying about them, and we saw my father start for the house as fast as he could travel. The bullets cut some small branches from the trees on our lawn, but the battle lasted only a few minutes and, so far as I know, no casualties occurred.

My sister Samantha, then a young girl of sixteen or seventeen, was so much impressed by this battle that a few days later she painted a picture of it from memory showing the Union infantry in their bright new uniforms and the Rebels on their horses. The major commanding the little body of cavalry had been quartered at our house for some weeks previous to the fight, so that his portrait is probably as true to life as the unskilled young artist could make it. Later this sister of mine studied under very fine artists in Cincinnati and did much excellent work in portrait and landscape painting." PIONEERING IN AGRICULTURE, ONE HUNDRED YEARS OF AMERICAN FARMING AND FARM LEADERSHIP, THOMAS C. ATKESON AND MARY M. ATKESON, 1937

Col. John A. Turley FREDERICK H. MESERVE, HISTORICAL PORTRAITS, NEW YORK STATE LIBRARY

Samantha J. Atkeson painted the scene below of the Battle of Atkeson Gate, fought September 26, 1862, near Buffalo, Putnam County, between Col. John A. Turley's 91st Ohio Volunteer Infantry and (probably) the 16th Virginia Cavalry under Maj. James H. Nounnan.

West Virginia Man Recorded Famed Rebel Yell

West Virginia is known for quite a number of Civil War "firsts," but one of the least known is that a West Virginian was the first and only person to ever record the famed "Rebel Yell," the familiar spine chilling battle cry of many a Confederate soldier. Generally speaking, even those with a remote knowledge of the Civil War have read of this "wildcat screech" which purportedly originated in 1861 on the battlefield of First Manassas (Bull Run) when the Confederate Army charged the Federal soldiers en masse and uttered that "high pitched yelp" when only a few yards from the Union battle line. This "fearful noise," a variation of a fox hunter's cry, became a Confederate trademark throughout the war and continually struck fear into the heart of many a Yankee soldier.

As expected, following the war many a writer attempted to put into words an accurate description of the 'rebel Yell,' but only Harvie Drew, formerly of the 9th Virginia Cavalry, C.S.A., came close when he said that if the yell could be spelled, it would sound something like "WHO — WHO–EY WHO–EY." He said the "WHO" was short and low, followed by a very high and prolonged "WHO" which ended on the "EY." And in order to resemble the actual yell it would have to be repeated at the same time at least a thousand times in order to be comparable to an army of charging rebel soldiers. Once the recording industry developed, it would have seemed a natural to attempt to make a phonograph recording of the yell by an ex–Confederate soldier, but such was not the case until 1929 by which time the ranks of the gray clad veterans had diminished drastically. But as it was, in 1929, the United Daughters of the Confederacy appointed a committee "To Secure a Phonograph Recording of the Rebel Yell," and member Mrs. Charles Reed of West Virginia was chosen to conduct that search. Oddly, the project continued unsuccessfully for five years, consuming much valuable time and research. Strange as it may seem, although there were yet many surviving Confederate veterans, they apparently could not find one who knew the yell.

By an even stranger quirk of fate, the motion picture industry unknowingly bailed out the U.D.C. project. In 1934 Metro–Goldwyn Mayer studios filmed a Civil War feature titled "Operator 13" which starred the highly popular Marion Davies. The producers desired realism for a scene involving a Confederate cavalry charge, and in their quest for an actual ex–rebel to make that sound, and apparently with more resources at hand than the U.D.C., located Sampson Sanders Simmons. It was he who purportedly accurately provided the famed war cry. MGM Pictures learned of the search by the U.D.C. and presented a copy of the recording to them, given in person by starlet Marion Davies. Regretfully, this was the first and only time a recording of the yell was made, and with the passing of the last Confederate veteran in 1957, there would never again be a man who could make the famous sound.

But the man who did immortalize that sound on record was a native of West Virginia. Sampson Sanders Simmons was born in what in now Cabell County, West Virginia. On March 20, 1862, he enlisted in Company E (Cabell County Border Rangers) of the 8th Virginia Cavalry. In 1863 he was wounded at Morristown, Tennessee, and he was captured at Moorefield, West Virginia, on August 7, 1864. From there he was sent to Camp Chase, the Federal prison camp at Columbus, Ohio, where he spent the remainder of the war. Reportedly, during his military service he had spent some time as a courier for Gen. "Jeb" Stuart.

Following the war Simmons moved to California where he became active in the Confederate Veterans group and was given the rank of General (having only been a Private during the war) and Commander–in–Chief of the Pacific Division. He was 90 years old when he recorded the "Rebel Yell," and at the age of 93 he dictated his memories to his daughter who had them published in 1954 with the title *Memories of Sampson Sanders Simmons: A Confederate Veteran.* The narrative was quite honest and included three postwar photos of Simmons in his uniform. Since his memoirs were published, at least two other postwar photos of him have been located and published in other books. One picture is an 1893 reunion of the Border Rangers at Greenbottom (the home of Gen. Albert Gallatin Jenkins, original captain of the Rangers) and the other a photo of him at the 75th Anniversary (Reunion) at Gettysburg. The old warrior passed away in 1942 at the age of 98 and was buried wearing his beloved Confederate uniform with a Confederate flag on his casket.

Now that all the old soldiers of the blue and the gray have indeed faded away, one of our only audible links with that great conflict in American history is an obscure recording made by a West Virginia Confederate veteran. It is reported that the national office of U.D.C. in Richmond, Virginia, is in possession of the recording and requests concerning it must be directed to them. Yet one other means of hearing it may exist if the movie "Operator 13" has not been destroyed by the ravages of time as have so many other films of that period. Wouldn't it be nice to sit in some dark theater watching this 1934 film of the Civil War and then be aroused out of our chairs when the voice of Sampson Sanders Simmons, West Virginia boy and ex–Confederate soldier, emanates the haunting "Rebel Yell?"

Terry Lowry

Carrying on the Memories

The war was over, but memories of the traumatic experiences lingered on. In 1866 Union veterans formed The Grand Army of the Republic, and in 1889 Confederate veterans formed the United Confederate Veterans. Many posts were established in West Virginia, but they eventually faded away by the 1950s. Today the Sons of Union Veterans and Sons of Confederate Veterans preserve the memories of their forefathers.

Women also had their Civil War organizations. Some Union veterans' wives and widows joined the GAR's auxiliary The Women's Relief Corps, and the Confederate women formed the United Daughters of the Confederacy in 1894. Many of the Confederate monuments in West Virginia were wholly or partially sponsored by the UDC. Today Union veterans' memories are preserved by the Daughters of Union Veterans of the Civil War.

Through the years, especially up to the first World War, veterans held many reunions through-

out the state. As the years stretched out, the reunions became infrequent. Perhaps the largest gathering of veterans from both sides since the Civil War occurred in 1913 for the 50th anniversary of the Battle of Gettysburg. Even in 1938, at the 75th anniversary of the great battle, over 1500 Union and Confederate veterans from all over the country attended.

The authors have chosen a number of reunion photographs from as many parts of the state as possible. Some of these reunions were of units that fought in the state but were not West Virginia units. Other reunions were of either state units or just groups of veterans from both sides who still lived in the state. This is especially the case in the 1913 Confederate reunion photograph taken in Huntington.

Reunion photographs will probably surface after this book is published and will, if available, be published in future editions.

4th West Virginia Infantry Monument Dedication at Vicksburg, Mississippi, November 1922. Bust is of Maj. Arza M. Goodspeed. Left to right: (1) unknown female; (2) Hugh Martindale - Adj. & Q.M. Gen. - represented G.A.R. Dept. of WV; (3) William Keely - represented WV Gov. - was 2nd Lt. and Post Q.M. 13th Maine Infantry - promo. to Lt. in 91st U.S. Inf.; (4) Phillip H. Elliott - 4th WVI; (5) Dr. J.J. Morgan - 4h WVI; (6) Mrs. H.S. White - Sec. of Vicksburg Mil. Park Commission and Pres. Ladies G.A.R. Dept. of WV; (7) possibly R.O. Sears - builder of monument; (8) H.S. White, Chairman, Vicksburg Mil. Park Commission; others unknown. VICKSBURG NATIONAL MILITARY PARK

Confederate veterans at an Ice family reunion in Marion County around 1900.

A Civil War veterans' reunion in Marion County around 1900.

The end of the Civil War did not bring a cessation of ill feeling between the participants in the war and the sympathizers for each side, but gradually time began to heal the sounds. Reunions were held, at first in military array but finally in civilian clothing, and eventually survivors from each side in the struggle were able to meet together in friendship. This group is shown reportedly meeting about 1880, although it appears to be a wartime photo.

The Meade Post No. 6, GAR Silver Drum Corps pose in front of their headquarters on Monroe Street in Fairmont in the early 1900s.

ALL PHOTOS TAKEN IN MARION COUNTY
AND COURTESY THOMAS KOON

Top: *Band reunion in Philippi.* Bottom: *Aging veterans, probably from Taylor County, pass in front of* the B&O *depot in Grafton, no date.* CITY OF PHILIPPI

Philippi is all decked out in these historic photos for Old Soldiers Day on the 50th anniversary of the 1861 Battle of Philippi. CITY OF PHILIPPI

This photo was taken on the steps of the old capitol building in downtown Charleston about 1910 by the well known Gravely Photographers. The men are members of R.E. Lee Camp No. 878, UCV of Charleston. Names are as follows: (1) James L. Kelley, Co. D, 8th Va. Cavalry; (2) D.C. Lovett, Co. C, 8th Va. Cavalry; (3) John Henry Wilson, Co. H, Kanawha Riflemen, 22nd Va. Infantry; (4) Preston Martin, Co. C, 36th Battalion, Va. Cavalry, (5) Veto Farrar, Co. A. 36th Va. Infantry; (6) George S. Chilton, Co. E, 22nd Va. Infantry; (7) Press Lanham, Co. A, 22nd Va. Infantry; (8) William J. Thomas, Jackson's Va. Battery; (9) James Z. McChesney, Co. F, 11th Va. Cavalry, transferred to Co. C, 14th Va. Cavalry; (10) James L. Jones, Co. A, Huger's Battery of Artillery; (11) John F. Ballard, Co. C, 22nd Va. Infantry; (12) William C. Hopkins, Co. E, 36th Va. Infantry; (13) Henry M. Brown, Co. B, 44th Va. Infantry; (14) John N. Hutchinson, Co. C, 36th Va. Infantry; (15) N.O. Sowers, Co. I, 2nd Va. Infantry, Stonewall Brigade; (16) Albert J. Wallen, Co. D, 12th Georgia Battery Artillery; (17) Elisha H. Merricks, Lowry's Va. Battery; (18) George W. Mays, Co. K, 24th Va. Infantry' (19) Pleasant Bailey, Co. A. 22nd Va. Infantry; (20) Samuel Motley, Co. A, 8th Va. Cavalry; (21) Henry D. McFarland, Kanawha Riflemen, Co. H, 22nd Va. Infantry. The man standing at the far left is Dr. Will Tompkins; the boy is Eugene Gleason. WEST VIRGINIA STATE
ARCHIVES

This photograph, reportedly taken in a Charleston drugstore shortly after the end of the war, appeared in the April 17, 1938, issue of The Charleston Daily Mail. *It shows a group of just–returned former officers of the "Kanawha Riflemen" in 1865. As the article's author George W. Summers stated, "Despite their beards evidently grown when shaving facilities were unknown in camp, these fellows were scarcely more than boys when the picture was made." Standing, left to right" Maj. Thomas L. Broun, Col. Thomas Smith, Samuel A. Miller, Col. William Fife, and Capt. Nicholas Fitzhugh. Seated, left to right: Dr. Joseph Watkins, Lt. William A. Quarrier, Capt. Richard Q. Laidley, and Capt. John Swann. The "Kanawha Riflemen" became Company H, 22nd Virginia Infantry, CSA, at the start of the war.* NATIONAL SOCIETY OF COLONIAL DAMES OF AMERICA, WEST VIRGINIA

Two views of members of the 23rd Ohio Volunteer Infantry band which was stationed for a time in the Kanawha Valley. They gathered at Lakeside, Ohio, August 20, 1885.
RUTHERFORD B. HAYES LIBRARY, HN 3501, HN 2520

The "Dixie Girls" pose together at a 1910 Confederate soldiers reunion in Franklin, Pendleton County. Left to right: Estelle Erick, Grace Hendrick, Myrtle Dyer, Nellie Hammer, Maggie Simmons, Nan Arbogast, Lillian Calhoun, Louise Hiner, Matie Colaw, Mollie Calhoun and Kittie Anderson. West Virginia State Archives/Bill & Harriet McCoy, Pendleton County Collection

This is the most famous photograph ever taken at White Sulpher Springs. Taken in August 1869, it is the only photograph of Robert E. Lee and a group of former Confederate generals. Lee is second from the left in the front row. The generals standing behind him are, left to right: James Conner of South Carolina, Martin Gary of South Carolina, J. Bankhead Magruder of Virginia, Robert Lilley of Virginia, P.G.T. Beauregard of Louisiana, Alexander Lawton of Georgia, Henry Wise of Virginia, Joseph Brent of Maryland. Seated in the front row, left to right: Blacque Bey, Turkish Minister to the U.S.; Lee; philanthropist George Peabody; banker W.W. Corcoran; Judge James Lyons. The Greenbrier Resort Archives

McNeill's Rangers reunion at Moorefield, Hardy County, August 31, 1910. Hardy County Library

In this September 27, 1910, photo, Confederate veterans march down Capitol Street, on their way to the unveiling of the bronze statue of Stonewall Jackson on the Capitol grounds, located in downtown Charleston. The statue was commissioned by the Charleston chapter of the United Daughters of the Confederacy and now stands on the southeast corner of the Capitol grounds. On the right, leading the parade with upright sword, is James Z. McChesney, commander of the R.E. Lee Camp 887 of the United Confederate Veterans Permission had been granted for these veterans to carry the battered flag of the old 22nd Virginia Infantry Regiment (formerly the "Kanawha Riflemen."), but in deference to the governor, who had given the permission, the veterans themselves would not carry the colors. West Virginia State Archives, Jan Hutchinson Abbott Collection

Logan County Wildcats, Co. C, 36th Virginia Infantry, CSA, get together in Logan. TERRY LOWRY COLLECTION

Confederate veterans of the Henry Kyd Douglas Chapter, UCV (or SCV) meet at Shepherdstown around 1900. JEFFERSON COUNTY MUSEUM

Original photo labeled: "Survivors of the Border Rangers, Co. E, 8th Virginia Cavalry, CSA." Back row, left to right: (1) James Dodson, (2) James D. Sedinger, (3) Leo Hendrick, (4) James Baumgardner, (5) Sampson S. Simmons, (6) B. Boothe, (7) A.A. "Gus" Handley. Front row, left to right: (8) Charles Shoemaker, (9) B.A. "Gus" Walcott, (10) Thaddeus W. Flowers, (11) W.E. Wilkinson, (12) Lucian C. Ricketts, (13) J.S. Stewart, (14) Geo. W. Hackworth. Photo taken February 22, 1893, by S.V. Mathews at Huntington, West Virginia. JACK DICKINSON VIA JAMES E. MORROW LIBRARY, MARSHALL UNIVERSITY

Last Confederate Reunion in Beckley

Eighty grizzled veterans in Gray attend annual State Reunion here last week. The annual reunion of West Virginia Confederate Veterans of the Civil War held in Beckley last Thursday was one of the most successful state gatherings of the rapidly thinning ranks of gray that has been held in many a year. The register at headquarters showed that a total of eighty of the remaining heroes of the lost cause living in this end of the state had journeyed for one more touch of elbows with the comrades in arms during the four terrible years when they endured untold hardships together.

That the reunion was a gladsome affair and afforded much pleasure to the old men was evident from the expressions on all their faces.

The complimentary dinner served at the Beckley Hotel was a delightful feature, not to the diners alone but to many local people who dropped in to witness the gathering. Their picture was taken, grouped about the Court House steps, and each man was presented with one of them.

Thomas Patton Shaver, the veteran standing on the right with saddle bags across his shoulder, brought this picture back from the Reunion. RALEIGH REGISTER, BECKLEY, WEST VIRGINIA, SEPTEMBER 12, 1918

PHOTOS COURTESY W.T. LAWRENCE
FAYETTEVILLE, WEST VIRGINIA

Civil War veterans gathered at Enon, Nicholas County, October 28, 1926. Left to right: George H.C. Alderson, William H.H. Neil, J.J. Halstead, Wyatt Meader, Jilson H. Neal, J.C. Loughary. CARNIFEX FERRY STATE PARK MUSEUM

Confederate veterans, some of whom were members of Camp Garnett, UCV, pose in Huntington, Cabell County. They were members of the 8th Virginia Cavalry. JACK DICKINSON

Photo of the Confederate Army veterans from Pocahontas County who attended the Confederate Reunion in Richmond, Virginia, May 30 through June 3, 1907. The photo was probably taken as the men waited to board the train in Marlinton on May 28. A number of ladies and sons of Confederate veterans also joined the approximately thirty county veterans at the reunion. Left to right: Levi Waugh, W. Crawford Hull, John Varner, Charlie L. Moore, George H. Hamilton, Preston N. Harper, Hugh P. McLaughlin, W.R. Brady, Jehue Trainer, A.C.L. Gatewood, William E. Hicks, J.J. Ripptoe, George H. McLaughlin, Aaron Jordan. Mr. Jordan was not a soldier but went through the Civil War as a servant to a Confederate officer.

POCAHONTAS COUNTY HISTORICAL SOCIETY VIA BILL McNEEL

Reunion of Confederate veterans at Parkersburg's city park, circa early 1920s. BLENNERHASSETT HISTORICAL PARK COMMISSION VIA PAUL A. BORRELLI

A group of Confederate veterans from Hampshire County, photographed in Romney about 1910. Front row: Inskeep, Kump, Houser, Montgomery. Second row: Meloney, White, Garrett, Parsons, Poling.

HAMPSHIRE COUNTY HISTORICAL SOCIETY

ANNUAL MEETING OF CONFEDERATE ENCAMPMENT OF W. VA.
HUNTINGTON, W. VA. OCT. 9 & 10 1913

Three sections of a panoramic image. In this panel, note famous feuder "Devil" Anse Hatfield, second man standing from left, with dark beard.

BILL WINTZ

West Virginia Civil War service medals, struck for every Union soldier from West Virginia.
WEST VIRGINIA STATE ARCHIVES

STATE'S GRATITUDE.

It is a remarkable fact, and one to be well thought of, that but two of the States that remained loyal to the Government in the recent civil war have given their soldiers medals to commemorate their services in the great struggle; these are Ohio and West Virginia. There can be no better or more enduring memento of the late civil strife than these tokens of a nation's gratitude. It is cause for regret that other States have not imitated the example of Ohio and West Virginia.

Some of the States are contemplating the erection of monuments to the memory of the great events of the war. While this is done, how gratifying would it be for each soldier still living, or the families of those whose lives were sacrificed for their county, to be possessed of these tokens of national gratitude! These little mementoes would find their way into the remotest sections of the whole country, and be handed down as heirlooms from generation to generation, and would do more good in creating a love of country than all the monuments that might adorn all the principal cities. These are not seen by those who inhabit the rural districts, from whence came the greater portion of the soldiery during the war. It is not too late yet for other States to do an act of patriotic justice, by at once turning their attention to a due consideration of this subject.

A contract for twenty-six thousand medals was completed a short time ago, for the West Virginia officers and soldiers, by Mr. A. Demarest, at 182 Broadway, New York, of which the engravings are fair representations:

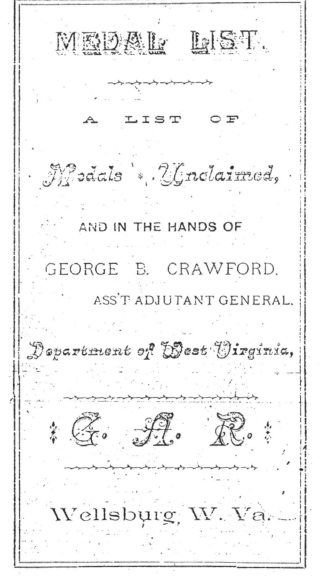

MEDAL LIST.

A LIST OF

Medals Unclaimed,

AND IN THE HANDS OF

GEORGE B. CRAWFORD.

ASS'T ADJUTANT GENERAL.

Department of West Virginia,

G. A. R.

Wellsburg, W. Va.

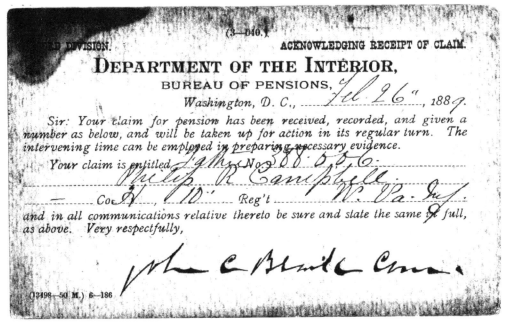

(3—040.)   ACKNOWLEDGING RECEIPT OF CLAIM.

LD DIVISION.

DEPARTMENT OF THE INTERIOR,
BUREAU OF PENSIONS,
Washington, D. C., _Feb 26"_, 188_9_.

Sir: Your claim for pension has been received, recorded, and given a number as below, and will be taken up for action in its regular turn. The intervening time can be employed in preparing necessary evidence.

Your claim is entitled _Sghts No 388.556._

Philip R Campbell

— Co. _H_, _10"_ Reg't _W. Va. Inf._

and in all communications relative thereto be sure and state the same in full, as above. Very respectfully,

John C Black Com.

(13498—50 M.) 6—186

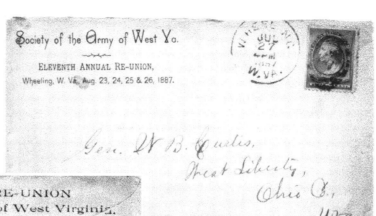

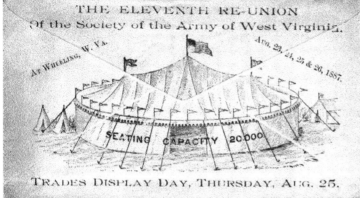

BILL WILCOX COLLECTION

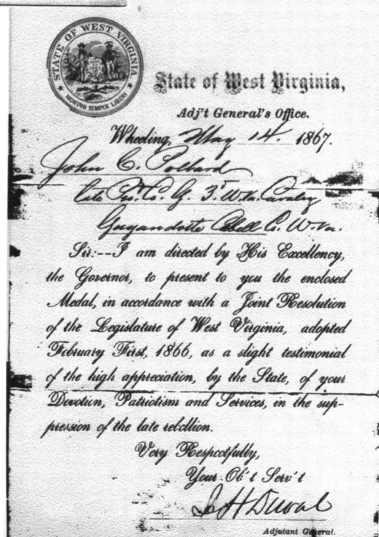

The Tenth Reunion of the Society of the Army of West Virginia

President, Major-General George Crook, U. S. A.

Vice-Presidents:

1. General R. B. Hayes,
2. General W. H. Powell,
3. General B. F. Kelley,
4. General I. H. Duval,
5. General R. H. Milroy,
6. General B. F. Coates.
7. General W. H. Enochs,
8. General Van H. Bukey,
9. Colonel J. M. Schoonmaker,
10. Captain J. P. Hart,
11. Major Alex Shaw,
12. Colonel Thayer Melvin,
13. Colonel Robert Bruce,
14. Major John W. Overturf,
15. Private Mark B. Wells,
16. Captain E. E. Ewing,
17. Major B. M. Skinner,
18. Captain C. W. Boyd.

AND THE SEMI-ANNUAL

Encampment of the Department of Ohio, G. A. R.

Tuesday, Wednesday, Thursday and Friday, Sept. 7th, 8th, 9th, and 10th, 1886.

Executive Committee:

E. E. Ewing, Chairman,
Dr. C. P. Dennis, Recording Secretary,
J. H. Simmons, Corresponding Secretary,
George D. Selby, Treasurer,
W. K. Thompson, } Committee
J. W. Lewis, } on Grounds
A. J. Finney. } and Privileges.

Dr. P. J. Kline,
John K. Duke,
M. B. Wells,
John W. Overturf,
Dr. A. Titus.
Committee on
G. A. R. Encampment.

⚜ INVITATION ⚜

Portsmouth, Ohio, July 1, 1886.

DEAR SIR:— You are cordially invited to be present at the Tenth Reunion of the Society of the Army of West Virginia, and the Mid-Year Encampment of the Department of Ohio G. A. R., to be held in this city.

Tuesday, Wednesday, Thursday and Friday, Sept 7, 8, 9 and 10, 1886.

Those who attended the Reunion here last year will testify to the good faith of our citizens in making good their promises, and we can offer the assurance that nothing will be left undone this year that will enhance the interest and enjoyment of all who attend.

We hope that you will be with us, and inform other comrades and bring them with you. All will be welcome.

J. A. TURLEY,
J. W. OVERTURF,
MARK B. WELLS,
H. R. TRACY,
E. E. EWING,
A. M. DAMARIN,
G. D. WAIT,

JNO. G. PEEBLES,
JNO. K. DUKE,
M. STANTON,
GEO. DAVIS,
G. D. SELBY,
W. A. CONNOLLEY,
P. J. KLINE,

J. G. REED,

COMMITTEE ON INVITATION.

HEADQUARTERS

DEPARTMENT OF WEST VIRGINIA,

GRAND ARMY OF THE REPUBLIC.

I. M. ADAMS,
DEPARTMENT COMMANDER.

A. J. CHARTER,
ASSISTANT ADJUTANT GENERAL,

SENIOR VICE COMMANDER,
T. S. WATSON,
MORGANTO'

JUNIOR VICE COMMANDER,
T. H. MARKS,
WELLSBI

DEPARTMENT CHAPLAIN,
TAYLOR RICHMOND,
R. F. D. 3, FAIRM(

MEDICAL DIRECTOR,
J. H. BROWNFIELD,
FAIRM(

QUARTERMASTER GENERAL,
J. B. MORGAN,
RAVENSW

JUDGE ADVOCATE,
COL. HENRY HAYMOND,
CLARKSB

Ravenswood, W. Va., July 30, 1907.

HONORABLE W. M. O. DAWSON,

    GOVERNOR OF WEST VIRGINIA,

        CHARLESTON, WEST VIRGINIA.

    SIR:-

    I have been instructed by the Department of West Virginia assembled at Fairmont, W. Va. last May to request you to deliver to competent persons whom we will select (with your approval) a few of the old but valued flags under which we fought from 1861 to 1865 so that they may be taken to Saratoga, N. Y. to the National Encampment, which meets there September, 9th. 1907.   We will care for them and return them as good as when we received them, they are ours we bought them with the lives of many of our comrades and not any one would care for them as we shall.   Hopeing for a favorable answer, I am,

            Yours truly,

              Department Commander

JAMES Z. McCHESNEY, COMMANDER
HENRY M. BROWN, ADJUTANT

HEADQUARTERS
R. E. LEE CAMP, No. 887

United Confederate Veterans

Charleston, W. Va. May 5th 1910

Capt Geo. S. Chilton

Dear Sir

Mr A. B. Jacks.

a member of Company E. 22d Regiment Virginia Infantry desires to become a member of this Camp and refers to you to vouch for him as a soldier true & loyal to the Confederacy until the end. Please write your voucher on the back of this letter. & sign it officially as Captain of your company

Yours fraternally

James Z. McChesney

APPLICATION FOR MEMBERSHIP.

To the COMMANDER, OFFICERS, COMRADES, CONFEDERATE VETERANS

OF

STONEWALL JACKSON CAMP No. 878, U. C. V.
Charleston, West Virginia.

Desiring to be of some service to the charitable objects as set forth in your By-Laws, I offer myself for membership, and if elected will comply with the By-Laws of the same. Herewith please find enclosed **$1.00** for Muster Fee, which I will expect returned if I am rejected.

I was born _7th_ day _Mach_ 18_43_ in _Rockbridge_ County,

State of _____ Enlisted _5_ day _November_ 186_2_.

Where _at Winchester Va_ By whom _Capt Alex G McChesney_

Company _7_ Regiment _17 Battl Va Cav afterward, 11 Va Cav_ Brigade _Robinsons Wm E Jones (Laurel Brig_

was at V M I Jany 62. With Cadets at McDowell Battle May 8 - 62.

Rank _Privat_ Promoted _____

Transferred _August 9 1863 at Brandy Station Va_ Captured _____

Remarks _to Co C 14th Va Cavalry Jenkins afterward McCausland Brigad Resigned from V M I in July to enlist the army & Served without pay with 17th Battl Cav until I enlisted regularly in Nov 62. Serves in 2 Manassas aug 62_

Honorably Discharged, Paroled _was on sick league at close of war, paroled at Staunton Sometime in June_

I hereby affirm that the above is a true record, as witness my hand and signature.

Signed (Full name signed) _James L McChesney_

Vouched for by member of this camp. P. O. _Charleston W Va_

Date _May 5th 1907_

Refer to war papers to Genl. Jno McCausland Grimms Landing W Va H. I H Stephenson Monterey Va

INCORPORATED UNDER THE LAWS OF
WEST VIRGINIA

SHARES $1.00 EACH

N⁰ 21

One Shares

Stonewall   **Jackson**

FULL-PAID

NON-ASSESSABLE

This Certifies That

CAMP

John Clark   is the owner of

One Share of the Capital Stock of STONEWALL JACKSON CAMP, not subject to Assignment, Sale, Pledge or Transfer.

In Witness Whereof, the duly authorized officers of this Corporation have hereunto subscribed their names and caused the corporate seal to be hereunto affixed, at Charleston, W. Va., this *11* day of *May* 190*8*.

J. W. Vickers Secretary   *J. J. Wilcox* President

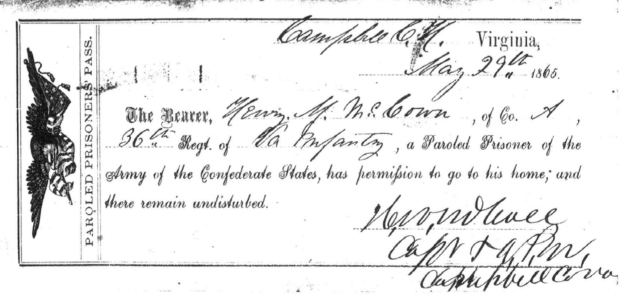

Campbell C.H. Virginia,
May 29th 1865.

The Bearer, *Henry M. McCown*, of Co. *A*, *36th* Regt. of *Va Infantry*, a Paroled Prisoner of the Army of the Confederate States, has permission to go to his home; and there remain undisturbed.

PAROLED PRISONERS' PASS.

Paroled Prisoners Pass of Henry M. McCown of Co. A, 36th Infantry, CSA. H.M. McCown was born near Buffalo in 1838 and died at Ashland, Kentucky, in 1913. He was a grandson of Malcolm C. McCown of Capt. Arbuckle's company at Pt. Pleasant, 1775-76, who later became a pioneer settler in the vicinity of Buffalo, and the son of Francis McCown who migrated from Ireland to Augusta County, Virginia, in 1740.

CONFEDERATE MEMORIAL ASSOCIATION

OFFICE OF
MAJ.-GEN. ROBERT WHITE,
MEMBER EXECUTIVE COMMITTEE.

Wheeling, W. Va. 18 Aug. 1897

CIRCULAR.

Headquarters West Virginia Division
United Confederate Veterans.

Wheeling, W. Va., August 18th, 1897.

Comrades:

A third of a Century has passed since the war was ended. The history of the Commands which were in the Confederate Army from the territory now West Virginia, remains yet to be faithfully and truthfully told.

Our dead, many of whom fell in battle, others who died in prisons, still lie, scattered, where first interred, in now almost forgotten graves.

The United Confederate Veterans must build their grand Memorial Hall and Temple.

In a few short years, all who now survive, will have passed away. Our present duty is sacred—we must "be up and at" our work. "The night cometh when no man can Work."

1. New camps should be formed throughout the State as rapidly as possible. Fifteen or more old soldiers can form a Camp. For information address Gen'l George Moorman, No. 824 Common St., New Orleans, La., or these Headquarters.

2. Each Camp is urged to see that not only the history of the respective commands to which its members may have been attached, but the history of each soldier who went to the war from the County in which the camp is located, be speedily written or printed, and copies furnished to these Headquarters for proper use in the publication of general history—Camps should be called together, committees appointed and means adopted to carry speedily forward this great work.

THIRTY-THIRD

Annual Encampment

Dept. West Va.

G. A. R.

At SISTERSVILLE, W. VA.

MAY 18th, 19th and 20th

HEADQUARTERS

DEPARTMENT,   HOTEL TYLER
W. R. C.   -   -   -   "   "
Ladies G. A. R.   -   -   "   "

BUCKHANNON
IS
BOOMING.

G. A. R. DAY,
April 22, 1891.

COMPLIMENTS OF

Buckhannon Land Trust
Association,

UPSHUR CO., W. VA.

PROGRAM

TUESDAY, MAY 18th.

Headquarters will be opened at 10 o'clock A. M., where all Comrades will register, receive their badges and be assigned to their lodgings.

Reception Committee will meet all incoming trains and escort Comrades and Ladies to headquarters.

2 o'clock P. M. Assemble at the City Hall. Music by the Band.

Call to order by T. G. Hammond, Department Commander.

Invocation by Department Chaplain.

7:30 o'clock Memorial Services for departed Comrades at the Baptist Church, corner of Wells and Hill streets, conducted by Department Chaplain and other speakers.

The public is cordially invited to this service.

WEDNESDAY, MAY 19th.

G. A. R. Assemble at City Hall. Music by the Band. Call to order by T. G. Hammond, Commander.

Invocation by Department Chaplain.

Address of Welcome by J. B. Scohy, Mayor of the city. Response by Department Commander or some other Comrade. Citizens and visitors are cordially invited to attend this service.

1:30 P. M. Business Session and exchange of greetings between Ladies of G. A. R., the W. R. C. and Grand Army.

2:30 o'clock. Grand parade of ex-soldiers, Headed by Sistersville Band and the Veterans Drum Corps, participated in by children of the City Schools, Sons of Veterans, Boy Scouts and Fraternal Organizations.

Parade will form on Brown Betty St. Route of Parade: Brown Betty to Charles, North on Charles to Wells, South on Wells to Catherine, North on Catherine to Water, up Water to Hill, East on Hill to Main, South on Main to Charles, East on Charles to Wells up Wells to Cemetery Road, Disband.

7:30 P. M. Campfire at City Hall, Conducted by Commander T. G. Hammond. Addresses and reminiscences by distinguished Comrades and Visitors. The public is cordially invited to attend this meeting.

THURSDAY, MAY 20th

9 A. M. Assemble at the City Hall.

Music by the Band.

Selecting Next Place of Meeting.

Election and Installation of Officers.

PETER LOY,
Chairman of Committee

FRANK LESLIE'S
ILLUSTRATED
NEWSPAPER

Entered according to Act of Congress, in the year 1887, by MRS. FRANK LESLIE, in the Office of the Librarian of Congress at Washington.— Entered at the Post Office, New York, N. Y., as Second-class Matter.

No. 1,669.—Vol. LXV.] NEW YORK—FOR THE WEEK ENDING SEPTEMBER 10, 1887. [PRICE, 10 CENTS. $4.00 YEARLY. 13 WEEKS, $1.00.

WEST VIRGINIA—THE BANNER INCIDENT AT WHEELING, ON THE OCCASION OF THE RECENT GRAND ARMY PARADE—VETERANS SWERVING FROM THE LINE OF MARCH TO AVOID PASSING BENEATH PRESIDENT CLEVELAND'S PORTRAIT.

FROM SKETCHES BY A STAFF ARTIST.—SEE PAGE 59.

Broadsides

and Miscellaneous Items

Communication during the Civil War, of course, was very primitive as compared to wars that followed. There were telegraphs, signal flags and newspapers, but to get the word out to the general populace in a certain area, broadsides were printed and put up in many public places for all to read.

These broadsides varied from recruitment posters to military orders pertaining to the general populace or political views and commentaries. A few newspapers—very rare military ones — are also included here. This is only a small portion of what is available, and an entire book could be made up of these alone. Also included is a sampling of letters, envelopes, orders and miscellaneous items used in the state during the war.

Men of Virginia!
MEN OF KANAWHA!
TO ARMS!

The enemy has invaded your soil and threatens to overrun your country under the pretext of protection.

You cannot serve two masters. You have not the right to repudiate allegiance to your own State. Be not seduced by his sophistry or intimidated by his threats. Rise and strike for your firesides and altars. Repel the aggressors and preserve your honor and your rights. Rally in every neighborhood with or without arms. Organize and unite with the sons of the soil to defend it. Report yourselves without delay to those nearest to you in military position. Come to the aid of your fathers, brothers and comrades in arms at this place who are here for the protection of your mothers, wives and sisters. Let every man who would uphold his rights, turn out with such arms as he may get and drive the invader back.   **C. Q. TOMPKINS,**
Col. Va., Vol's. Comdg.
Charleston, Kanawha, May 30, 1861.

Col. Christopher Q. Tompkins was a prominent citizen of the Gauley Bridge area prior to the war. He was commissioned a colonel of Virginia volunteer forces in the Kanawha Valley in 1861 at the age of 47. This broadside is a good example of the intense feeling of part of the area's population early in the war and the efforts of the authorities to repel the invasion of the Federal soldiers. Tompkins resigned from the service in November 1861.

Head-Quarters Department of the Ohio,

CINCINNATI, MAY 26, 1861.

TO THE UNION MEN OF WESTERN VIRGINIA:

The General Government has long enough endured the machinations of a few factious Rebels in your midst. Armed traitors have in vain endeavored to deter you from expressing your loyalty at the polls. Having failed in this infamous attempt to deprive you of the exercise of your dearest rights, they now seek to inaugurate a reign of terror, and thus force you to yield to their schemes, and submit to the yoke of the traitorous conspiracy, dignified by the name of Southern Confederacy. They are destroying the property of citizens of your State, and ruining your magnificent railways. The General Government has heretofore carefully abstained from sending troops across the Ohio, or even from posting them along its banks, although frequently urged by many of your prominent citizens to do so. It determined to await the result of the late election, desirous that no one might be able to say that the slightest effort had been made from this side to influence the free expression of your opinion, although the many agencies brought to bear upon you by the rebels were well known. You have now shown, under the most adverse circumstances, that the great mass of the people of Western Virginia are true and loyal to that benificent Government under which we and our fathers have lived so long. As soon as the result of the election was known, the traitors commenced their work of destruction. The General Government can not close its ears to the demand you have made for assistance. I have ordered troops to cross the river. They come as your friends and brothers—as enemies only to the armed rebels who are preying upon you. Your homes, your families, and your property are safe under our protection. All your rights shall be religiously respected.

Notwithstanding all that has been said by the traitors to induce you to believe that our advent among you will be signalized by interference with your slaves, understand one thing clearly—not only will we abstain from all such interference, but we will, on the contrary, with an iron hand, crush any attempt at insurrection on their part.— Now, that we are in your midst, I call upon you to fly to arms and support the General Government. Sever the connection that binds you to traitors—proclaim to the world that the faith and loyalty so long boasted by the Old Dominion, are still preserved in Western Virginia, and that you remain true to the Stars and Stripes.

GEO. B. McCLELLAN,

Major General U. S. A., Commanding Department of the Ohio.

McClellan was a major figure in the early 1861 West Virginia campaign and went on to command Union forces in 1862 (the Peninsula campaign and the Battle of Antietam.) In 1864 he ran for President as a Democrat against Abraham Lincoln.

TO THE PEOPLE

Of the Department of the **KANAWHA VALLEY**, embracing the following Counties, viz: Mason, Jackson, Putnam, Cabell, Wayne, Logan, Kanawha, Boone, Wyoming, Raleigh, Fayette, Nicholas and Clay: According to the following order, by the

Governor of Virginia:

Executive Department, April 29, 1861.

LIEUT. COL. McCAUSLAND:

Sir: You will proceed at once to the Kanawha Valley and assume command of the volunteer forces in that section, and organize and muster the same into the service of the State; and as soon as they are formed into Battalions or Regiments, report the fact to me, with the names of the company officers, the number of men in each company, and the kind and quality of arms.

Gen. Lee will give all necessary orders for your government in that command. I am very respectfully,
JOHN LETCHER.

I have arrived here to take command of the Department. I have instructions to call into the field ten companies, and one company of artilery. These troops will be encamped in the Kanawha Valley, near Buffalo, Putnam Co. They are intended for the protection of the Department; and I appeal to the people of the border counties to abstain from anything which will arouse ill feeling on either side of the Ohio river. This Department is organized by the proper authority in the State, and is provided with the credit to sustain itself; but for complete success, I firmly rely on the friendly disposition of the people therein.

The volunteer companies of the counties of Mason, Jackson and Putnam, will rendezvous at **BUFFALO**, Putnam Co.

The volunteer companies of the counties of Cabell, Wayne, and Logan, will rendezvous at **BARBOURSVILLE**, Cabell county.

The volunteer companies of the counties of Kanawha Boone, Wyoming, Raleigh, Fayette, Nicholas and Clay, will rendezvous at **CHARLESTON**, Kanawha county.

The Captain of the volunteer companies in the above counties will remain at their respective drill grounds, until ordered to their rendezvous by the Commandant of the Department. So soon as preparation to receive them can be made, the companies will be ordered to their respective rendezvous, mustered into the service of the State, and then ordered to the Camp of Instruction. No company will be mustered into service unless it has at least 82 men.

The Captains will see that each man is provided with a uniform, one blanket, one haversack, one extra pair of shoes, two flannel shirts (to be worn in the place of the ordinary shirts), two pairs of drawers, four pairs of woolen socks, four handkerchiefs, towels, one comb and brush and tooth-brush, two pairs white gloves, one pair of rough pantaloons for fatigue duty, needles, thread, wax, buttons, &c., in a small buckskin bag. The whole (excepting the blanket) will be placed in a bag, this bag will be placed on the blanket and rolled up, and be secured to the back of each man by two straps.

Lt. Col. JNO. McCAUSLAND,
Commanding Dep't Ka. Valley.

John McCausland rose to the rank of general in the Confederate army. He fought all over the state and became rather notorious for his burning of Chambersburg, Pennsylvania, in 1864. At the end of the war he refused to take the oath of allegiance to the United Stated and became known as the "unreconstructed" rebel. He eventually settled on his farm in Mason County and was the second to last Confederate general officer to die, in 1927.

RIPLEY, VIRGINIA,
July 6th, 1861.

To the true and loyal citizens of Western Virginia, and particularly those on the Ohio border, I would earnestly appeal to come to the defense of the Commonwealth, invaded and insulted as she is by a ruthless and unnatural enemy. None need be afraid that they will be held accountable for past opinions, votes, or acts under the delusions which have been practiced upon the Northwestern people, if they will now return to their patriotic duty and acknowledge their allegiance to Virginia and her Confederate States as their true and lawful sovereign. You were Union men, so was I, and we had a right to be so until oppression and invasion and war drove us to the assertion of a second independence. The sovereign State proclaimed it by her Convention and by a majority of more than one hundred thousand votes at the polls. She has seceded from the old and formed a new Confederacy; she has commanded and we must obey her voice. I come to execute her commands, to hold out the olive branch to the true and peaceful citizens, to repel invasion from abroad and subdue treason only at home. Come to the call of the country which owes you protection as her native sons!

HENRY A. WISE,
Brig. Gen'l.

Henry Wise was an ex-governor of Virginia and became a brigadier general in the Confederate army at the start of the war. He commanded a portion of the troops (Wise Legion) in the disastrous Kanawha Valley campaign in 1861 and had many problems with his co-commander Gen. John Floyd. Wise was later sent to command troops in South Carolina.

GENERAL ORDER.

HEAD QUARTERS,
DEPARTMENT OF WESTERN VIRGINIA,
Charleston, Va., Sept. 24, 1862.

General Order, No.

The money issued by the Confederate Government is secure, and is receivable in payment of public dues, and convertible into 8 per cent. bonds. Citizens owe it to the country to receive it in trade; and it will therefore be regarded as good in payment for supplies purchased for the army.

Persons engaged in trade are invited to resume their business and open their stores.

By order of   MAJ. GEN. LORING.
H. FITZHUGH
Chief of Staff.

To the People of West-ern Virginia.

The Army of the Confederate States has come among you to expel the enemy, to rescue the people from the despotism of the counterfeit State Government imposed on you by Northern bayonets, and to restore the country once more to its natural allegiance to the State. We fight for peace and the possession of our own territory. We do not intend to punish those who remain at home as quiet citizens in obedience to the laws of the land, and to all such clemency and amnesty are declared; but those who persist in adhering to the cause of the public enemy, and the pretended State Government he has erected at Wheeling, will be dealt with as their obstinate treachery deserves.

When the liberal policy of the Confederate Government shall be introduced and made known to the people, who have so long experienced the wanton misrule of the invader, the Commanding General expects the people heartily to sustain it not only as a duty, but as a deliverance from their taskmasters and usurpers. Indeed, he already recognizes in the cordial welcome which the people everywhere give to the Army, a happy indication of their attachment to their true and lawful Government.

Until the proper authorities shall order otherwise, and in the absence of municipal law and its customary ministers, Martial Law will be administered by the Army and the Provost Marshals. Private rights and property will be respected, violence will be repressed, and order promoted, and all the private property used by the Army will be paid for.

The Commanding General appeals to all good citizens to aid him in these objects, and to all able-bodied men to join his army to defend the sanctities of religion and virtue, home, territory, honor, and law, which are invaded and violated by an unscrupulous enemy, whom an indignant and united people are now about to chastise on his own soil.

The Government expects an immediate and enthusiastic response to this call. Your country has been reclaimed for you from the enemy by soldiers, many of whom are from distant parts of the State, and the Confederacy; and you will prove unworthy to possess so beautiful and fruitful a land, if you do not now rise to retain and defend it. The oaths which the invader imposed upon you are void. They are immoral attempts to restrain you from your duty to your State and Government. They do not exempt you from the obligation to support your Government and to serve in the Army; and if such persons are taken as prisoners of war, the Confederate Government guarantees to them the humane treatment of the usages of war.

> By command of
>
> MAJ. GEN. LORING.
> H. FITZHUGH,
> *Chief of Staff.*

HEAD QUARTERS, DEPARTMENT OF WESTERN VIRGINIA,
CHARLESTON, VA., September 14, 1862.

General Order No.

The Commanding General congratulates the Army on the brilliant march from the Southwest to this place in one week, and on its successive victories over the enemy at Fayette C. H., Cotton Hill, and Charleston. It will be memorable in history, that overcoming the mountains and the enemy in one week, you have established the laws, and carried the flag of the country to the outer borders of the Confederacy. Instances of gallantry and patriotic devotion are too numerous to be specially designated at this time; but to Brigade Commanders, and their officers and men, the Commanding General makes grateful acknowledgment for services to which our brilliant success is due. The country will remember and reward you.

> By command of
>
> MAJ. GEN. LORING.
> H. FITZHUGH,
> *Chief of Staff.*

The Confederate army, under Maj. Gen. W.W. Loring occupied the Kanawha Valley for a brief period in September 1862. Many of the troops under his command were native to the area, and it would be their last visit until the end of the war.

Head Quarters,

DEPARTMENT OF SOUTH-WESTERN VIRGINIA,
SALT SULPHUR SPRINGS, August 1862.

GENERAL ORDERS, No.

By direction of the General Commanding is hereto appended a list of those absent without leave from the 2nd Brigade of this Command. All such absentees are ordered to report to their respective Regiments, Battalions or Companies within ten days from the publication of this order. Those so reporting within this period will be assigned to duty without further trial. Those failing to report within the prescribed limit of time will be proceeded against as deserters. The absentees from Maj. Jackson's Battalion of Cavalry will be allowed fifteen days to report.

By Order of   Maj. Gen. W. W. LORING.
August 20th, 1862.   W. B. MYERS, A. Adjt. General.

A List of Men absent from the 8th Va. Cavalry.

B. F. Aiken,	R. B. Diggs,	Andrew Greer,	William Lacy,
John P. Aiken,	Kinser,	Henry Davis,	Sampson Simmons,
J. W. Anderson,	Smith,	Stephen F. Jones,	J. B. Beckwith,
W. Anderson,	Spencer,	D. A. Taylor,	Simonton,
J. Anderson,	Coleman,	C. Wesley,	W. W. Hamilton,
D. W. Bean,	Kidd,	J. Cossett,	J. Ralsin,
J. H. Copenhaver,	Peerry,	Wm. M. Boone,	T. R. C. Blankinship,
S. M. Copenhaver,	Thornhill,	J. W. Bowyer,	W. H. Russel,
Wm. E. Copenhaver,	Fitzpatrick,	Wm. R. Thornton,	A. Hornbert,
W. W. Thompson,	Ferguson,	A. J. Woodall,	Edwin Lambert,
J. Park,	Stewart,	H. Davidson,	Paul C. Smith,
Thomas Copenhaver,	Jones,	Fletcher,	J. W. Harman,
A. B. Cook,	Staples,	Muse,	Wm. C. Sogner,
A. P. Cole,	Ballon,	A. B. Nash,	J. E. Maurice,
John J. Hester,	Spencer,	J. D. Morton,	M. B. Ranbirne,
S. T. Morrison,	Joseph Faber,	J. B. Perdue,	William Stevens,
L. G. Maupin,	H. A. Bourn,	S. W. Sinclair,	J. Strader,
J. M. Saunders,	J. D. Pickett,	Ely,	J. J. Stafford,
J. L. Thomas,	J. Austin,	Thompson,	A. T. Snyder,
James R. Evans,	William Austin,	A. P. Handley,	P. R. Snyder,
James Nuckles,	Martin Nelson,	P. M. Russel,	W. G. Panley,
Thomas Smith,	Henry Nelson,	J. V. Ralson,	J. P. Lambert,
John C. Hite,	M. Honk,	J. E. Shelton,	T. P. Hereford,
James W. Mathews,	E. W. Greer,	A. Page,	William A. Smith.

J. M. CORNS,   A. C. BAILEY,
 Col. 8th Va. Cavalry.   Adjt. 8th Regt. Va. Cavalry.

STATE OF VIRGINIA.

ISSUED BY AN ACT OF THE CORPORATION OF APRIL 30TH, 1861.

1   DOLLAR.   Charlestown, January 1, 1862.   DOLLAR.   **1**

No. *1095*   DUE BY   G.

THE CORPORATION OF CHARLESTOWN,
ONE DOLLAR,

Payable in current funds by _____ Treasurer, to the Bearer, on presentation of these Bills in sums of Five Dollars.

_____ Clerk of the Board.   _____ Prest.

POST OFFICE DEPARTMENT.

JOHN H. REAGAN,

Postmaster General of the Confederate States of America.

TO ALL WHO SHALL SEE THESE PRESENTS, GREETING:

Whereas, On the 6th day of *January* 1862, *Peter P. Warnstaff* was appointed *Postmaster* at *Sweedlin Hill* in the County of *Pendleton*, State of *Virginia* ; and whereas he did, on the 21st day of *February* 1862, EXECUTE A BOND, and has taken the OATH OF OFFICE, as required by law,

Now know ye, That, confiding in the integrity, ability, and punctuality of the said *Peter P. Warnstaff* I do commission him a Postmaster, authorized to execute the duties of that Office at *Sweedlin Hill* aforesaid, according to the LAWS OF THE CONFEDERATE STATES, AND THE REGULATIONS OF THE POST OFFICE DEPARTMENT: To hold the said Office of Postmaster, with all the powers, privileges and emoluments to the same belonging, during the pleasure of the Postmaster General of the Confederate States.

In testimony whereof, I have hereunto set my hand, and caused the seal of the Post Office Department to be affixed, at *Richmond, Virginia*, the *fourth* day of *March* in the year of our Lord one thousand eight hundred and sixty-*two*.

John H. Reagan

POSTMASTER GENERAL.

Confederate States of America.

POST OFFICE DEPARTMENT,
APPOINTMENT BUREAU.

~~Montgomery~~, *Mch 4* 1862

SIR :

Your official bond and oath of office having been received and placed on file, I have the pleasure, herewith, to forward your commission.

Respectfully,

Your obedient servant,

W. M. Clements
Chief of Appointment Bureau.

The Confederacy still had inroads into that part of Virginia which would soon become a separate state. This was an appointment by Confederate Postmaster General John Reagan to a Peter Warnstaff to become the postmaster at Sweddlin Hill, Pendleton County. One wonders if he ever took his post, and if so, how long he held it? DR. NORVAL RASMUSSEN, MORGANTOWN, WEST VIRGINIA

Confederate States of America,
POST OFFICE DEPARTMENT,
OFFICIAL BUSINESS.

W. M. Clements
CHIEF OF THE APPOINTMENT BUREAU.

Peter P. Warnstaff Esqr
Sweedlin Hill
Pendleton Co.
Virginia

TO THE LOYAL CITIZENS
OF THE
KANAWHA VALLEY.

The 8th REGT. VA. VOL. INFANTRY has returned to the Kanawha Valley. This regiment served as the advance guard of Fremont's army in the Valley of Virginia, and was several times complimented by Gen. Fremont in General Orders, for its gallantry in action and behavior on marches. Afterwards it became a part of Sigel's corps, and after performing an honored part in the bloody campaigns of the Rappahannock, and participating in the Bull Run fight, it hastened back to Western Virginia, eager to assist in driving the rebel hordes from their homes and yours.

Having been in service nearly eighteen months, its ranks are much thinned. Half its term of service has expired, and you are now appealed to, to come forward and volunteer to fill up the ranks for the rest of the term.

All who wish to enter the service of their country, with veteran troops, and under officers of experience and tried courage, have now a glorious opportunity. You will receive the same pay, bounty, clothing, &c., as in any other regiment. Come on, then, loyal men of Virginia! Range yourselves side by side with your friends and brothers, and drive the ruthless Rebels from your so..!

COALSMOUTH, Dec. .. 1862

This broadside, issued at Coalsmouth, St. Albens, December 1862, called for volunteers for the 8th Regiment Virginia Volunteer Infantry, a Union regiment.

FELLOW-CITIZENS, OF WOOD COUNTY:

It having been represented to me, that if I became a candidate for the Clerkship of the Circuit Court of this county, there would be no Union candidate against me. I consented to be a candidate; but it being certain, that there is another Gentleman, (Union) running for the office, and not wishing to divide the Union vote, I hereby decline, and request my friends to vote for the Union candidate. I am not a candidate.

W. HATCHER.

Parkersburg, Va., Dec. 10, 1862.

		Value of Pro'y $	Amount of Tax. cts.
Mr. *Jno. S. Brady*			
TO COUNTY LEVY, AUGUST TERM, 1862.			
Bounty for Volunteers U. S. Army, from Monongalia County.			
To $1.30 per cent. on Land Tax, $	*10.41*		
To $1.30 per cent. on Personal Property, $	*4.56*		*14.96*
Received Payment,			
	JAMES ODBERT, S. M. C.		

GENERAL ORDERS—

No. 28. The General Commanding has been repeatedly pained to learn that a few bad men in some of the Regiments of his command, are in the habit of abusing, beating, and otherwise maltreating the negro and mulatto servants and teamsters employed by officers and quartermasters in his command. The services of these negroes and mulattos are necessary and cannot be dispensed with, without taking soldiers from their legitimate duties, which would be an injury to the service. These black people are generally quiet and orderly—they were created black and cannot help it—they have mostly been made slaves, and robbed of the proceeds of their own labor, and could not help it; and have left traitor masters in arms against our forces, and are desirous of helping us all they can; and are, therefore, entitled to our pity and commiseration, rather than abuse and contempt; and none but traitors or a coward who would strike a woman and abuse children would wantonly maltreat them. It is suspected that the rebels have hired these bad men to enlist in some of our regiments as spies, and for the purpose of abusing and driving back the contrabands, that they (the rebels) may have the benefit of the services of their slaves, and they be deterred from coming into our lines.

It is therefore ordered, and hereby made the duty of *every officer and soldier* of this command, to *immediately shoot down* every soldier or other person, who may be found causelessly abusing, beating, or otherwise maltreating any of the negro or mulatto servants, or drivers in or about this command.

By order of

BRIGADIER GENERAL R. H. MILROY.

HENRY C. FLESHER,
Capt. & A. A. A. Gen.

*This unusual broadside was posted by Brig. Gen.
R.H. Milroy, commander of Union troops in the
Cheat Mountain Division (central and eastern West
Virginia) on October 22, 1862.*

No. 142   Confederate States of America,

Lewisburg, Va   Office,
March 22   1864

This will Certify, That Joseph McMillion
has paid in at this office Five Hundred Dollars,
for which amount Registered Bonds, of the Confederate States of America, bearing interest from this date, at the rate of four per cent. per annum, will be issued to him, under the "act to fund and limit the currency" approved February 17, 1864, upon the surrender of this Certificate at this office.

500$

John Withrow,
Depositary.

Although Greenbrier County's loyalties leaned toward the Southern cause, this receipt is unusual for being issued so late in the war and still inscribed as Lewisburg, Virginia, rather that West Virginia.

HEAD-QUARTERS,
4th WEST Va. Vol. Inf't.
GALLIPOLIS O. APRIL 26, '64

THE UNION FOREVER!

SPECIAL ORDERS NO. 2.

1st. By orders received from the Superintendent of Recruiting Service for West Virginia, the Fourth West Virginia Veteran Vol. Inf't., will rendezvous at

GALLIPOLIS, MAY 1st. '64.

Officers, and enlisted men of the Command, will report prom_dy on said day.

2d. Head-Quarters of the Regiment for the present,

AT CAPT. JNO. A. ROBINSON'S STORE,
ON THE LOWE_ _IDE OF PUBLIC SQUARE.

BY ORDER OF
Lieut. Col. VANCE.
Commanding Regiment.

JAMES W. DALE,
1st Lieut. and acting Adjutant.

Headquarters Military District of Harper's Ferry,

Harper's Ferry, Va., November 17, 1864.

GENERAL ORDERS, No. 23.

The General Commanding publishes this order for the information of all whom it may concern.

The Government of the United States having rebuilt the railroad from Harper's Ferry to Winchester, Va.—To protect the same from molestation from guerillas and disloyal citizens along the line of same, the General Commanding, instructed by the Major General Commanding, in the event that the operations of said railroad are interfered with by guerillas or disloyal citizens, "To arrest all male secessionis's in the towns of Shepherdston, Charlestown, Smithfield, and Berryville, and in the adjacent country, sending them to Fort McHenry, Md., there to be confined during the war; and also, to burn all grain, destroy all subsistence, and drive off all stock belonging to such individuals,—turning over the stock so seized to the Treasury Agent for the benefit of the Government of the United States."

Upon the contingency arising requiring the execution of the instructions herein set forth, the same will be executed promptly and thoroughly.

By order of BRIG. GEN. STEVENSON.

S. F. ADAMS,

A. A. A. General.

OFFICIAL:

Notice that this Union army order listed Harpers Ferry as being in Virginia. The boundaries as we know them today did not include the three counties on June 20, 1863.

Office Provost Marshal, Martinsburg, Va. 1864
Guards and pickets will pass John D Nadenbousch
on Dry Run road. good for days
Description—Age height complexion
Eyes hair
H. L. Karr
Capt. & Provost marshal
BY ORDER COL. GEO. D. WELLS, COMMANDING POST.

THE GUERILLA.

DEVOTED TO SOUTHERN RIGHTS AND INSTITUTIONS.

Vol. 1.   CHARLESTON, VA., OCTOBER 3, 1862.   **No. 6**

THE GUERILLA,

IS PUBLISHED EVERY AFTERNOON
By the Associate Printers.

TERMS—TEN CENTS per copy, or FIFTY CENTS per week.

Rates of Advertising.

One square, (10 lines,) first insertion 50 cents. Each subsequent insertion, - - - - 25 "

Advertisers will please mark the number of insertions wanted on the MS., or they will be continued until ordered out, and charged accordingly.

FOR THE GUERILLA.

TO ****.

I THINK OF THEE.

I.

I think of thee when twilight shade
Hath spread its mantle o'er the day,
To hide the sunbeams from our view,
And clothe the earth in silver grey.
I think of all thy virtues sare—
Thy beauty, grace and winning ways,
And humbly breathe a fervent prayer
That God may bless thee all thy days.

II.

I think of thee, when Luna sheds
Her mystic light down from above ;
And basking 'neath her mellow beams,
I realize the heart's first love.
And then when thoughts recall the past—
The joyous scenes of other years—
I sigh because I knew thee not,
Till sighing fills my eyes with tears.

III.

I think of thee at midnight hour,
When all on earth is hushed to rest,
And try to drive away the care
That dwells within my troubled breast.
And when in sleep I seek repose,
And strive to ease my aching heart,
Some idle dream will bring thee close,
And make my restless spirit start !

IV.

I think of thee when morning's light
Bids the darkness disappear ;
And in dreamy visions bright
I see thy gentle spirit near.
I think of no one else but thee,
For no one else is half so dear ;
Then if in battle I should fall !
Shed for me a single tear.

"WILTON."

Camp near Charleston, Oct. 1st, 1862.

A TALE OF TERROR.

At the "Crow Inn," at Antwerp, some years ago, a white spectre was seen bearing a lamp in one hand, and a bunch of keys in the other—this unpleasant visitor was seen by a variety of travelers, passing along a corridor.

Nothing would satisfy the neighbors that an unfortunate traveler had not been, at some period or other, despatched in that fatal room by one of the previous landlords of the house ; and the hotel gradually obtained the name of the "Haunted Inn," and ceased to be frequented by its old patrons.

The landlord finding himself on the brink of ruin, determined to sleep in the haunted room, with a view of proving the groundlessness of the story. To make the matter more sure, as he said, he caused the hostler to bear him company, on pretence of requiring a witness to the absurdity of the report ; but, in reality, from cowardice. At dead of night, however, just as the two men were composing themselves to sleep in one bed—leaving another which was in the room untenanted—the door flew open, and in glided the white spectre !

Without pausing to ascertain what it might attempt on approaching the other bed, towards which it directed its course, the two men rushed naked out of the room, and by the alarm they created, confirmed more fully than ever the evil repute of the house.

Unable longer to sustain the cost of so unproductive an establishment, the poor landlord advertised for sale the house in which he and his father before him were born and had passed their lives. But bidders were as scarce as customers ; the inn remained on sale for nearly a year, during which, from time to time, the spectre reappeared.

At length an officer of the garrison, who had formerly frequented the house, and recollected the excellent quality of its wine, moved to compassion in favor of the poor host, undertook to clear up the mystery by sleeping in the aforesaid haunted chamber ; nothing doubting that the whole was a trick of some envious neighbor, desirous of deteriorating the value of the freehold in order to become a purchaser.

His offer having been gratefully accepted, the captain took up his quarters in the fatal room, with a bottle of wine, and a brace of loaded pistols on the table before him ; determined to fire at whatever object might enter the doors.

At the usual hour of midnight, accordingly, when the door flew open and the white spectre, bearing a lamp and a bunch of keys, made its appearance, he seized both his pistols, when, fortunately, as his finger was on the point of touching the trigger, he perceived that the apparition was no other than the daughter of his host, a young and pretty girl, evidently walking in her sleep. Preserving the strictest silence, he watched her set down the lamp, place her keys carefully on the chimney place, and retire to the opposite bed, which, as it afterwards proved, she had often occupied during the lifetime of her late mother, who slept in the room.

No sooner had she thoroughly composed herself, than the officer, after locking the door of the room, went in search of her father and several competent witnesses, including the water bailiff of the district, who had been the loudest in circulating rumors concerning the Haunted Inn. The poor girl was found quietly asleep in bed, and her terror on awaking in the dreaded chamber afforded sufficient evidence to all present of the state of somnambulism in which she had been entranced.

From that period the spectre was seen no more ; partly because the landlord's daughter shortly after removed to a home of her own ; and the tales of horror so freely circulated to the bewilderment of the poor neighbors, ended in the simple story of a young girl walking in her sleep.

ALWAYS BE PREPARED FOR DEATH.—This was the admonition of a Missouri elder, as he placed in his son's belt two bowie-knives and a pair of revolvers.

TO KILL MOSQUITOS.—Chain their hind legs to a tree, then go round in front and make faces at them.

A SPLENDID CHANCE.

A FLYING BATTERY is about to be formed for *Gen. Jenkins' Cavalry Brigade,* to be officered by experienced artillerists, and to be equipped in the most superb style. The Battery is to consist of two three-inch rifled guns, two twelve pound howitzers, (light, such as the Richmond Howitzer Battalion has,) and two mountain rifled guns, to be packed, when necessary, on horses.—Fleet, active horses for the pieces are now being purchased by the Quartermaster of Jenkins' Brigade, and all necessary steps for the procurement of a complete outfit are being taken. Applicants for membership will be required to undergo a medical examination, and must be *young, active and intelligent.* The cannoneers will be mounted, and must furnish their own horses, which will be valued and paid for.

While it is expected to recruit the men from among the mounted companies now forming in this section, transfers can doubtless be procured for a few enterprising men from the regiments and battalions.

The service is a brilliant one, full of exciting incident. *No half-asleep men need apply!* A Recruiting Sergeant may be found for the present at the ORDNANCE OFFICE in Charleston.

Only two copies are known of The Guerilla, *which was published in Charleston during the Confederacy's short occupation of the Kanawha Valley in September 1862.*

Kanawha Valley Star.

The Kanawha Valley Star *was founded at Buffalo, Putnam County, in 1855 as* The Star of the Kanawha Valley. *It moved its office to Charleston in 1857 and expanded the Democratic, pro-Southern cause. Publisher John Rundle, a member of the Kanawha Riflemen, joined the Confederate army in 1861. Union troops confiscated his press when they occupied Charleston in July 1861.*

The Charleston Daily Bulletin *was published in 1864 by E.T. and S. Spencer Moore. The Moore brothers were also job printers, and The S. Spencer Moore Company in Charleston lasted over 100 years.*

VOL. VII. KANAWHA C. H., VIRGINIA, TUESDAY, MAY 21, 1861. NO. 5.

CHARLESTON
Daily Bulletin.

Charleston, W. Va., June 13, 1864. { 7 o'clock, Evening.

Vol. I. No. 11.

MOORE & BROTHER, Publishers.

Office, "Bank of the West" Building.

Terms (in advance).

For Single copy,   5 cents.
For One Week, delivered by carrier, $1 03
For One Month,

RATES OF ADVERTISING.

One Square (10 lines), or less, one insertion,   50 cents.
one week, $1 00
one month,   3 00

Two Squares, one month,   5 00

Monday, June 11, 1864.

Thurman's Guerrillas.—Their Captain Captured.

The train, consisting of half a dozen old and empty wagons, sent out with 35 men of the O. N. G. as a guard, for the purpose of gathering up the broken-down wagons on the road between Gauley and Meadow Bluff, met with misfortune on Friday morning near Sewall Mountain.

The wagon-master, Dan. Lee, of the 12th Ohio, hearing of the presence of Thurman's guerrillas when at the foot of Sewall, proposed to leave the train with a guard, and with the rest of the force go up to the top and see if any were to be found. Some eight of them, having horses, were in the advance, —the infantry following as fast as they could, when, arriving on top of Big Sewall, they saw two mounted rebels and charged upon them. But these were a bait, and four of our boys, including the wagon-master, soon found themselves surrounded by Thurman's entire company, who, upon their refusing to surrender, fired upon them. Their horses being shot under them, three of them escaped to the woods and got away safely; but nothing has been heard of the fourth, Private Joseph Johns, of Comp. II, 12th O. V. I. We fear he was killed.

The guerrillas followed as far as where the train had been left, but being disappointed in finding any plunder there, they burned the wagons and returned.

Two of the members of the 23d O. V. I. belonging to the train, having secreted themselves until the following day, were fortunate enough, having merely side-arms, to capture Capt. Bill Thurman, the notorious leader of this gang. He is now under guard.

Late intelligence from General Crook is to the effect that he is operating disastrously to the rebels. How and where, it is not deemed proper to publish at present.

BY TELEGRAPH.

THIS MORNING'S DISPATCHES.

Grant changing his Bas

Official Advices from Sherm

FURTHER FROM BUTL

Gen. Smith driving Marmadu

A Battle near Cynthiana

DAILY BULLETIN.   3

BY TELEGRAPH.

Fort Darling Captured!

The Enemy Repulsed by McPherson, leaving 2500 on the field!

Morgan Repulsed at Frankfort!

BURBRIDGE ROUTS MORGAN AT CYNTHIANA!

From General Butler.

NEW YORK, June 13, 1864.

The Herald's correspondent sends the following:

WHITE HOUSE, June 11.—News from the front this morning is most cheering. Two officers who have just arrived here, bring the joyful news of the capture of Fort Darling.

An order conveying this intelligence was read to the army last evening, and the cheers of our soldiers could be heard miles around.

From General Sherman.

NEW YORK, June 13, 1864.

The attack on McPherson proved very disastrous to the enemy. The rebels came on in two divisions, with great resolution, but were met with a very destructive fire of artillery and musketry. The fight continued for nearly an hour, when the enemy retreated, leaving the field covered with their dead and wounded, numbering nearly 2500.

After five days' fighting, principally on his own hook, McPherson has closed upon our right wing, enabling us to make important movements.

Latest from Morgan.

LOUISVILLE, Ky., June 12.

Dr. Whaler, U. S. Mail agent, who has been at Frankfort during the siege, left there at 4:30 this morning, and reports that fighting commenced at 6 o'clock Friday evening, lasting till dark, and continued at intervals during the night; the enemy approaching from Georgetown, in two forces, aggregating 1200. Seven hundred entered Old Frankfort, and five hundred entered New Frankfort. They had no artillery.

A small 4-pounder had been placed below the fort to protect our rifle-pits, which was captured by the rebels, but was subsequently retaken.

On Saturday firing continued from 7 o'clock in the morning to 3 o'clock in the afternoon, with short intervals. The rebels made two demands during the day for the surrender of the fort, both of which were refused by Col. Monroe of the 22d Kentucky, commanding

the fort; the rebels abandoned the attack at 4 o'clock on Saturday afternoon.

By 7 o'clock in the evening they were moving eastward. Our loss was 6 wounded, one of whom seriously. The rebel loss is unknown.

The fort was garrisoned by 150 Federals, only 12 of whom were soldiers. No injury was done to Frankfort, except burning the barracks and a bridge 3 miles northward.

Capt. Dickson, of Gen. Burbridge's staff, telegraphs to Gen. Ewing at Lexington at 9:35 P. M., that Burbridge completely routed Morgan's command at Cynthiana this afternoon.

Notice that the date for this newspaper is June 20, 1863, the first day for the new state of West Virginia, but the masthead still lists Morgantown as in Virginia. ALL NEWSPAPERS FROM WEST VIRGINIA STATE ARCHIVES

Top: Untitled landscape 1861 "Confederate scouts observing a union encampment on the Gauley."
Middle: Untitled wagon train scene in western Virginia.
Bottom: Untitled "Two sharpshooters."

William D. Washington volunteered for service in the Confederate army, where he served as a noncombatant in the present area of West Virginia, particularly in the Gauley River and Sewell Mountain regions. He was probably associated with the 51st Virginia Infantry, as John Hunter Jr., a university student attached to the regiment as a drill master, recorded in his diary from Sewell Mountain on October 9, 1861:

Went to top of a high mountain near camp and had a delightful view—the rich colors exhibited in the changing foliage on the mountain . . . in every direction made an entrancing picture . . .[William D.] Washington took some fine sketches from this point. The pure mountain air was very . . . delightful— we could catch the sounds of martial music from the camp below. Breastworks had been thrown up all around the brow of the mountain towards the enemy's camp. The tents pitched on the adjacent mountainside presented a fine picture for an artist and Washington was a true artist.

Hunter later joined Capt. James McDowell Carrington's Company, Virginia Light Artillery, or Charlottesville Artillery.

Washington's art featured "serene landscapes" which reflected "the sincerity of his own perspective." At the war's end he painted *The Burial of Latane,* and four years later copies of it would hang in "countless southern parlors, a symbol of the poignancy of a cause forever lost."

After the war he painted portraits of three Confederate generals—Stonewall Jackson, Robert E. Lee and Robert E. Rodes—which hang at Virginia Military Institute. In 1869 he was made professor of fine arts at the school but he died the following year.

THE SOCIETY OF THE ARMY OF
WEST VIRGINIA

BILL WINTZ COLLECTION

Original painting of Camp Reynolds by John W. Oswald of the 23rd Ohio V.I.

RUTHERFORD B. HAYES LIBRARY

About the Authors

Terry Lowry was born in 1949 and is a 1967 graduate of South Charleston High School where he worked on the school newspaper. He graduated in 1974 with a B.A. in History from West Virginia State College and later studied Civil War history at Marshall University Graduate School. He has been a professional musician since 1966 as well as contributing music editor for *The Charleston Gazette*, 1970-75, music editor for *The Charleston Gazette*, 1977-78-75,and with the circulation department of *The Atlanta Journal* for two years.

Lowry published his first book, *The Battle of Scary Creek: Military Operations in the Kanawha Valley, April-July 1861* in July of 1982. He has since published *September Blood: The Battle of Carnifex Ferry (1985);* and two volumes in the Virginia Regimental Series *22nd Virginia Infantry* (1988) and *26th (Edgar's) Battalion Virginia Infantry* (1991), and *Last Sleep: The Battle of Droop Mountain November 6, 1863* (1996). Additionally his Civil War articles have been published in *North South Trader, Wonderful West Virginia,* and *Confederate Veteran* magazines, as well as the *West Virginia Hillbilly*. He has also been a contributor to the *Time–Life* series of books and remains an avid collector of Civil War memorabilia.

Lowry was employed for 20 years with the circulation department of Charleston Newspapers, Inc. He is currently historian/curator at the Craik–Patton House, Charleston.

Stan Cohen was born in Charleston and is a graduate of Charleston High School and West Virginia University with a BS degree in geology. He has worked in the oil fields of West Virginia and as a geologist with the U.S. Forest Service in Montana and Alaska. After many years in the ski business and as a consulting geologist, he established Pictorial Histories Publishing Company in 1976. His first book was *The Civil War in West Virginia, a Pictorial History*. Since then he has authored or coauthored 68 books and published over 250. He specializes in Civil War and World War II books and has traveled the world visiting military sites and attending military reunions.

Through the years Cohen has been involved in the esbablishment of several museums and has helped many TV, movie studios, magazines, newspapers and book publishers with photos and information about historical topics.

CIVIL WAR BOOKS BY STAN COHEN

The Civil War in West Virginia, A Pictorial History
    West Virginia's Civil War Sites and
    Related Information
Hands Across the Wall, the 50th and 75th Reunions
    of the Gettysburg Battle
Bullets and Steel, The Fight for the Great Kanawha
    Valley, 1861-65, with Bill Wintz and Richard Andre
John Brown, The Thundering Voice of Jehovah
    A Pictorial Heritage
The General and the Texas, A Pictorial History of the
    Andrews Raid, April 12, 1862

OTHER CIVIL WAR BOOKS PUBLISHED BY PICTORIAL HISTORIES PUBLISHING COMPANY

Unreconstructed Rebel, The Life of General John McCausland C.S.A. by Michael J. Pauley
Jenkins of Greenbottom by Jack L. Dickinson
Diary of a Confederate Sharpshooter, The Life of James Conrad Peters by Jack L. Dickinson
Civil War Memoirs of Two Rebel Sisters by Bill Wintz
Civil War in Cabell County, West Virginia 1861-1865 by Joe Geiger Jr.
The Civil War in Fayette County, West Virginia by Tim McKinney
Robert E. Lee and the 35th Star by Tim McKinney
Robert E. Lee at Sewell Mountain: The West Virginia Campaign by Tim McKinney
West Virginia Civil War Almanac by Tim McKinney
Rise of the Ironclads by George Amadon
To Take Charleston by James Hagy
A Pictorial Encyclopedia of Civil War Medical Instruments and Equipment in three volumes by Gordon Dammann
A Pictorial History of Civil War Era Musical Instruments and Military Bands by Robert Garofald and Mark Elrod
John Brown Mysteries Jean Libby, Editor